AF412318

YOU KNOW WHERE I'M AT AND I KNOW WHERE YOU'RE AT
GARY HILL & MARTIN COTHREN

The letters of Martin Cothren have been transcribed character for character inclusive of all punctuation or the lack thereof. Spaces between sentences range from one to five and have been approximated.

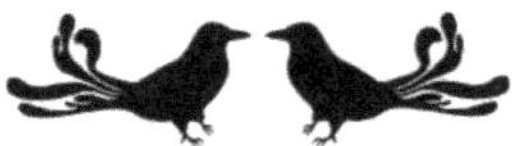

Encounters

*Cover & drawings** Martin Cothren
Graphic Design Gary Hill

Special Thanks Danièle Rivière, Valentine Leÿs Legoupil, Alina Zhak,
Mark McLoughlin, Akiem Helmling, Magdalena Hill,
Anastasia Hill, Christelle Fillod, Joseph C. Roberts,
Susan Quasha, Jean-Philippe Cazier, Vincent Lecocq,
Fabienne Leclerc, Paul Buck & Yakama Nation

* all *Untitled* (inks, ballpoint pen, graphite)- circa 1997 - 2014

Series **Encounters**
Directed by Danièle Rivière

In the same series:
- **School Spirit**
  by Pierre Huyghe & Douglas Coupland
- **Spread wide**
  by Kathy Acker, Paul Buck, John Cussans, Rebecca Stephens
- **Ubiq – a mental odyssey**
  by Mathieu Briand & Daniel Foucard
- **Have you ever seen a nomad in a hurry?**
  by Gilles Clément & Thierry Fontaine

www.disvoir.com/an/col/collection/2.Htm
www.facebook.com/groups/disvoir/

in memory of
Martin Cothren

Extend your arms in front of you and cross your left hand over your right (Fig. 1). Rotate your wrists (left hand clockwise/right hand counterclockwise) until the thumbs of both hands are approximately facing down. Clasp your hands together alternating the fingers from each hand (Fig. 2). Next bring your clasped hands towards your chest (Fig. 3) and keep turning your hands until they are directly in front of your face (Fig. 4). Now ask a friend to point to one of your fingers without touching it and try to lift the specified finger immediately. The complexity of this task will be frustratingly apparent as one attempts to move the selected finger.

1

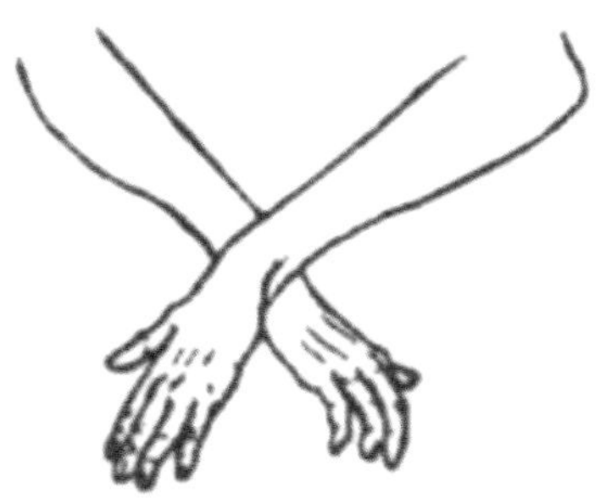

2

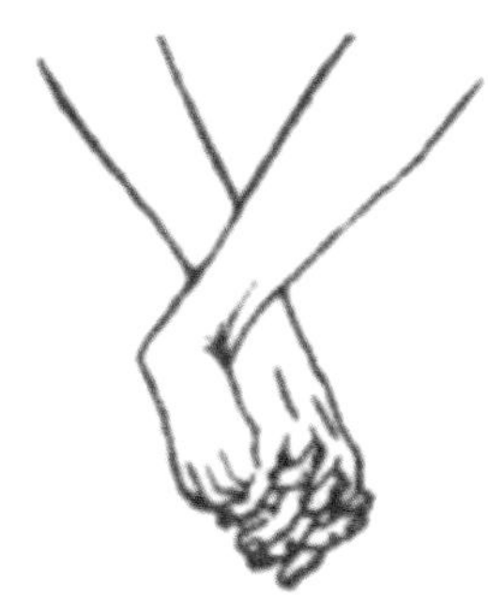

3

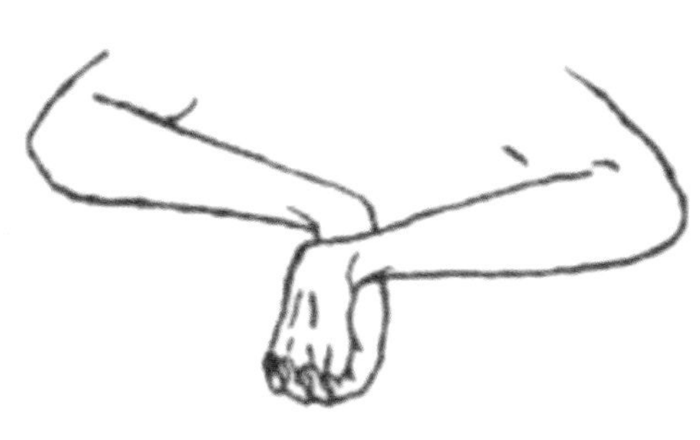

4

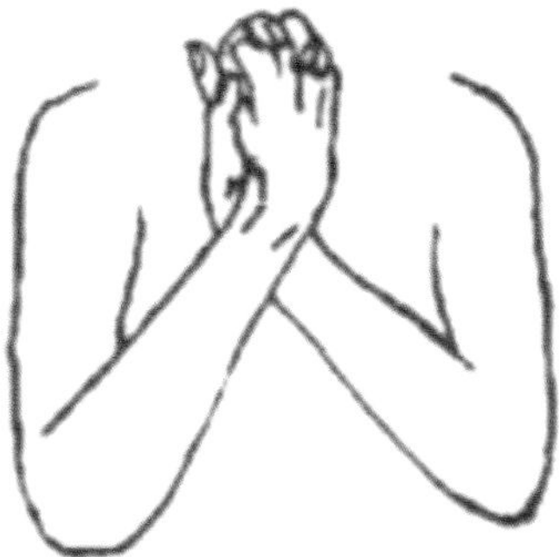

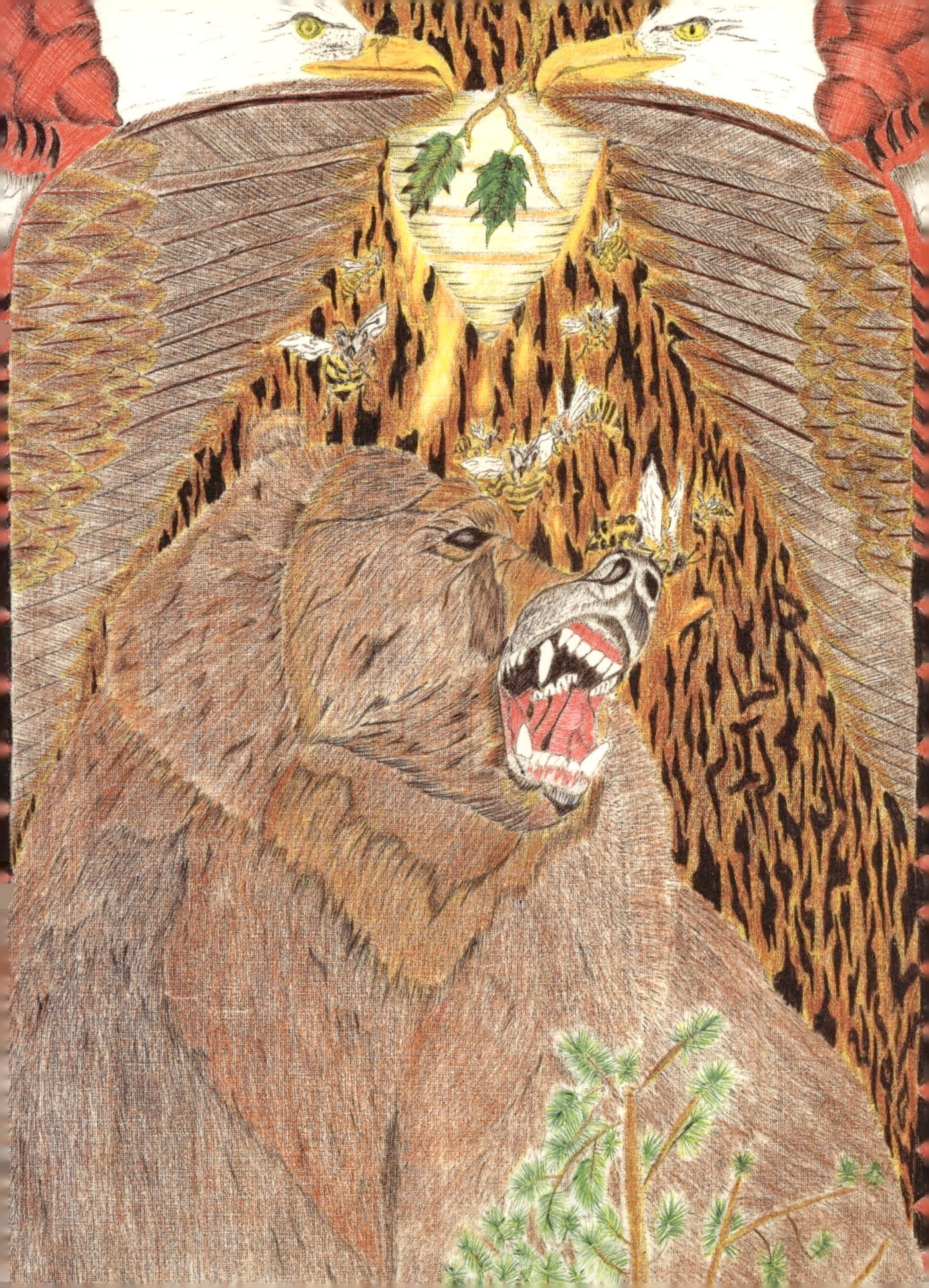

Gary

How it going. I hope this letter finds you well. I finely got out of the hole
Thank whoever spirit that got me out. So are you getting ready to take off to
your new gig, i hope so take in some good waves huh. Use your word Gig.
It sounds better from you. So did you all enjoy your meal or Celebration you
had for your daughter

Peopl are strange here   fire in my Ears Bro   We must get together n visit it
would be nice to see you finely it's been awhile

Here a number you can call n see if your approved on the visiting list 360-
794-2600   You leaving again it ok if you can't visit. So how is your new book
going   I've been talking to people here   They say it's proubly my last chance
Here in this joint   send me back to Walla Walla   So your weion ^women sick
hope she feeling better   Sometimes it's good to be sick, you realize how
good it feels to be well or sometimes you don't even realize the feeling   you
kno what i mean   Some people do not feel life to many other things goin
on   I went in to sweat on Sat did a couple round's   been outside most of the
days i've been here. Caught a cold here one day gone the next   You can't
have food sent in any more but we can order from in here   strange way they
do thing's sometimes. Sent my broken glasses back their wiped out. I've been
just hiding out in here being low key.   So your about to take off again be
careful Good Luck safe journey   Thanks for the cash. I hope we can delete
this tape. There will be no more minutes   Don't like the eariness. I will close
for now take care gary   I kno your my frind i don't care if you were green or
purple your my frind

Martin Cothren 955171 B-2-26
Monroe Correctional Center
Washington Reformatory ~~P.O. Box 777~~
P.O. Box 777
Monroe, Washington 98272

I'am reading The Lone Ranger Mister
it's alright

Thanks for The Book

Gary Hill
80th Vine St 101
Seattle Wash 98121

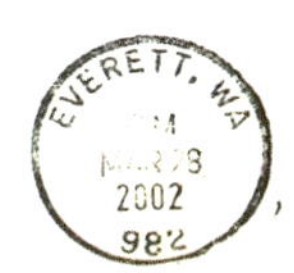

I would never have imagined befriending a person the likes
of Martin. In his own words, somewhat ironically, he was a
jail bird, a con, criminal, prison bum, your homeless lonely
convict, broke ass "frind," bro. It couldn't have been simply
that we worked together, given the brevity of time—one day,
actually just a few hours. Two months after that he was on
his way to prison. It would be easy to chalk it up to fate but
I found myself through the years turning over every possible
stone, pebble and grain of sand hoping to find an inkling as
to what would keep me entangled with the "Indian".... Is there
something to "like attracts like?" Were we somehow two sides
of some coin I haven't yet discovered?

Perhaps the trove lay in childhood where signs are always
abundant arising anywhere along the crisscrossing scribbles
of a life's directionality. With my father all but out of the
picture, my formative years were guided by my mother who
seemingly threaded a needle to make ends meet for my brother,
grandmother and me.

She worked as a full-time secretary at the UCLA medical
center; I was left to my own devices to get to and from school.
As inconsequential as they were, my first recollections of
Franklin Elementary were across the board. I wrote the word
"birthday" on the inside of my arm during a spelling test
and got busted in front of the whole class—I felt my face
turn crimson red. And then there was the little accolade for
my crayon drawing of a bear in the forest. The truly lasting
impression was getting hit in the face with a kickball. Not a
big deal save for the fact I was wearing glasses which made for
a real bloody mess. I made my way to the nurse's office holding
my face and slivers of glass: Just about every girl I passed in the
hallway let out a blood curdling scream which didn't exactly
make matters better.

My brother and I could have gotten away with murder, yet,
for whatever reason, we were mostly good (which is not to say
we were pussies either). In those days no one would think twice
about a 7-year-old going to the bowling alley on a mundane
Saturday afternoon.

Good Mourning it's Monday mourning about **6:45** I am still here
I woke up early about way before daylight listening to some person in the vent talking. Felt a stabbing pain in my chest. Started to think if I die! Please don't try to prevent my death let me fade away like the seasonal flower that leave us every year.

Or let there be light in my life. There is no joy in this place, it's all good. time fades away like a flower

In a leaf is a tree when the weather changes. Death chases all of us from beginning to the end. Its open like **7/11 24** hr a day Ha! Ha! "Early Mourning Thoughts"

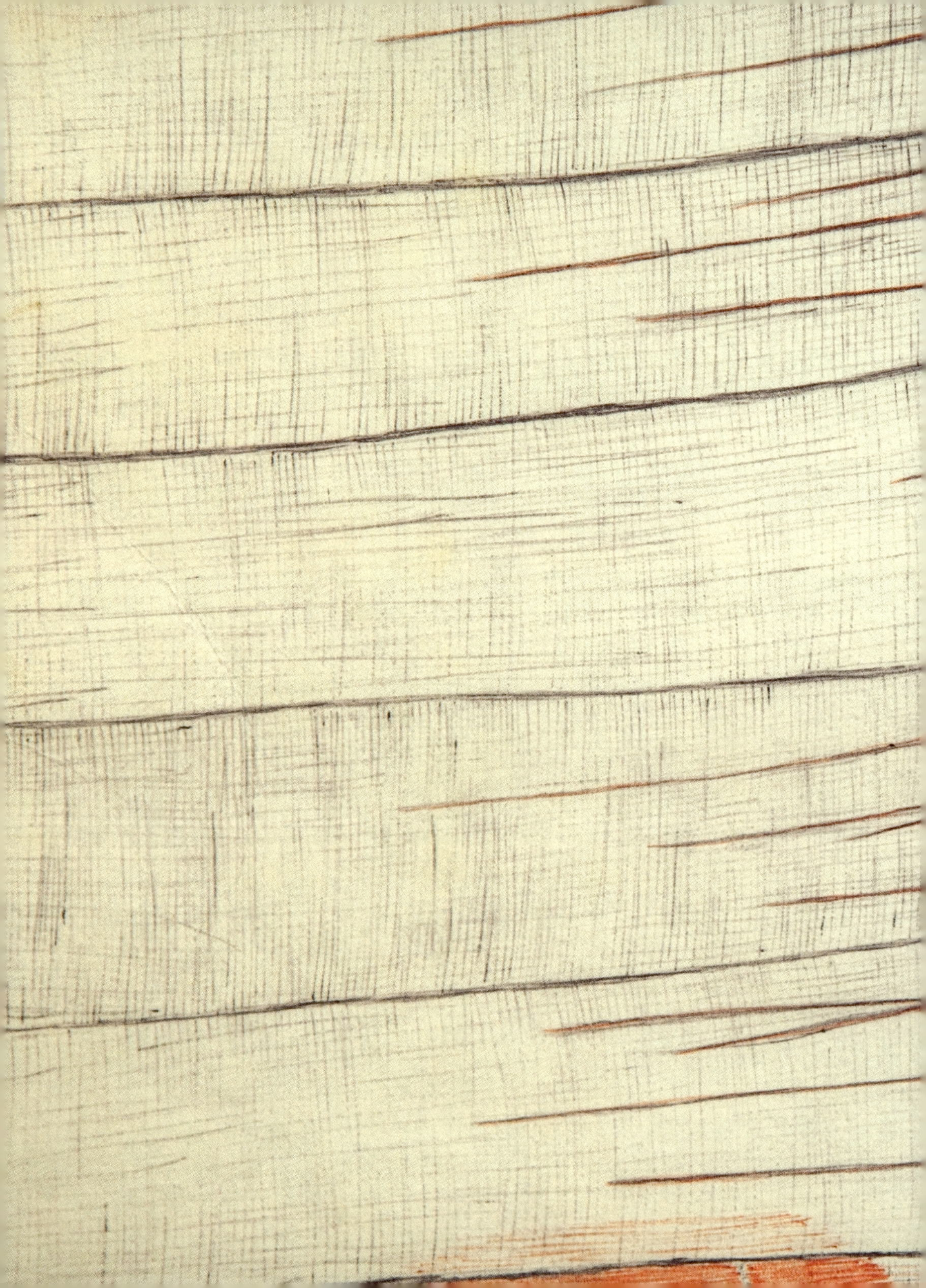

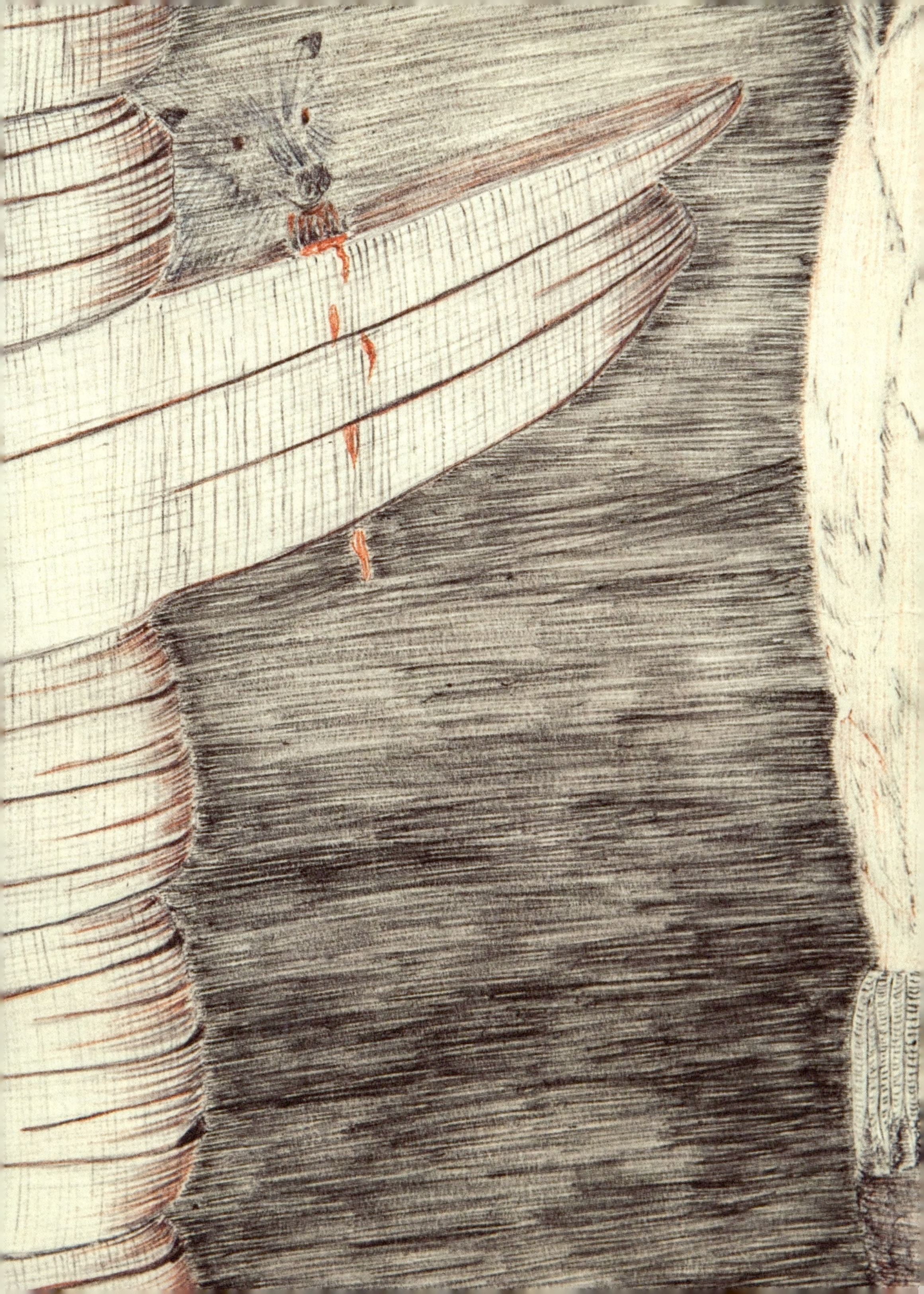

One time I was with a friend when a stranger offered to take us to his place and concoct a few homemade fireworks. Who knows what the lanky man had in mind, regardless he was cut off at the pass; my playmate who'd declined the invitation informed my mother of my approximate whereabouts. I figured I'd pop back home at the agreed upon time—no harm, no foul. "Never take candy or a ride from a stranger!" I favored the innocent excuse of parent/child signals getting crossed. For my mother? I've never seen her angrier, and rightfully so! To this day I don't know if he was a pedophile or an innocent man wanting to show us kids a good time. These scenarios are often mistaken for the worse. Reminds one of the film Sundays and Cybele. *This was one of maybe three times I got "the brush"—the pinnacle of punishment as far as my mother was concerned. It was the one unspoken fear both me and my brother had until one day when we were both to get it: we put books in our pants and as my mother began her discipline, the sound was not as it should've been. We started cracking up soon to be followed by our mother, who couldn't contain herself. There we were, all laughing hysterically at the bizarre scene. From that day on the brush had no teeth, and yet, goodness had been mysteriously instilled. How did she do that?*

We grew up in a small apartment complex in the heart of Santa Monica, a beachfront suburb of Los Angeles. My brother and I shared a bedroom in what would normally be used for a dinette next to the kitchen. My mother and her mother had the one bedroom down the hall. "Hattie," though I called her grandma, and I spent a considerable amount of time together, just the two of us. She was a Christian Scientist and read the bible daily. To complicate matters, she was a diabetic which meant it was God's will that she developed gangrene and had to have her leg amputated. We watched TV shows mornings and afternoons—the Little Rascals, Amos n' Andy, Sky King, The Twilight Zone—too many to name them all. I'd be lounging on the navy-blue carpet and she'd pull up in her wheelchair to watch the shows. Together we consumed the "box of glow," poorly camouflaged with a botched Bauhaus design, a desperate attempt at sci-fi furniture or a bad caricature of some Disney cartoon. On occasion I caught myself staring at her leg; the skin neatly tucked into the stump looked all too much like a giant anus. It haunted me for the few remaining years of her life. Like many a kid, especially from the west ('is the best'), Cowboys and Indians were paramount and The Lone Ranger, along with Tonto and Silver were ever-present. Through the early years I had many cap guns—six shooters with holsters, rifles and harmless bow and arrow sets. The sling shot was unwittingly the most dangerous. I kept it hidden under my bed with other items of secrecy.

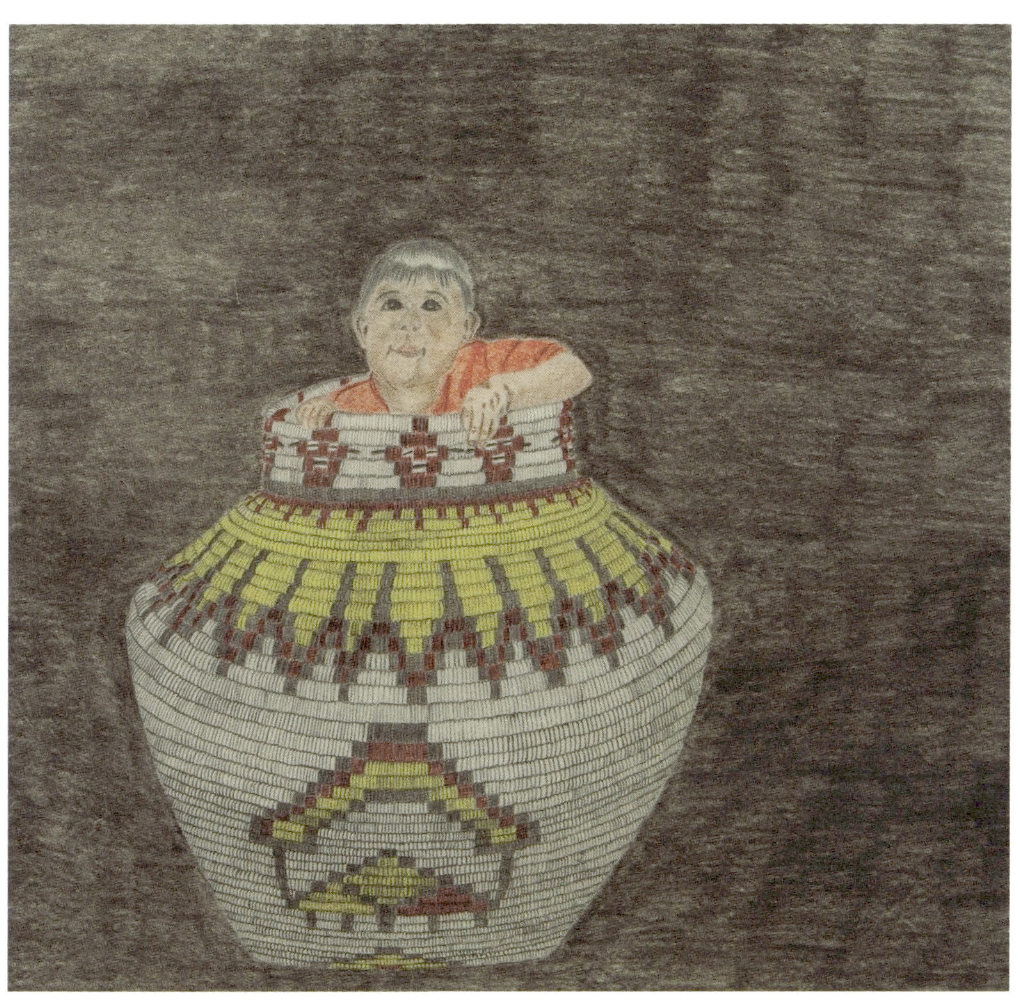

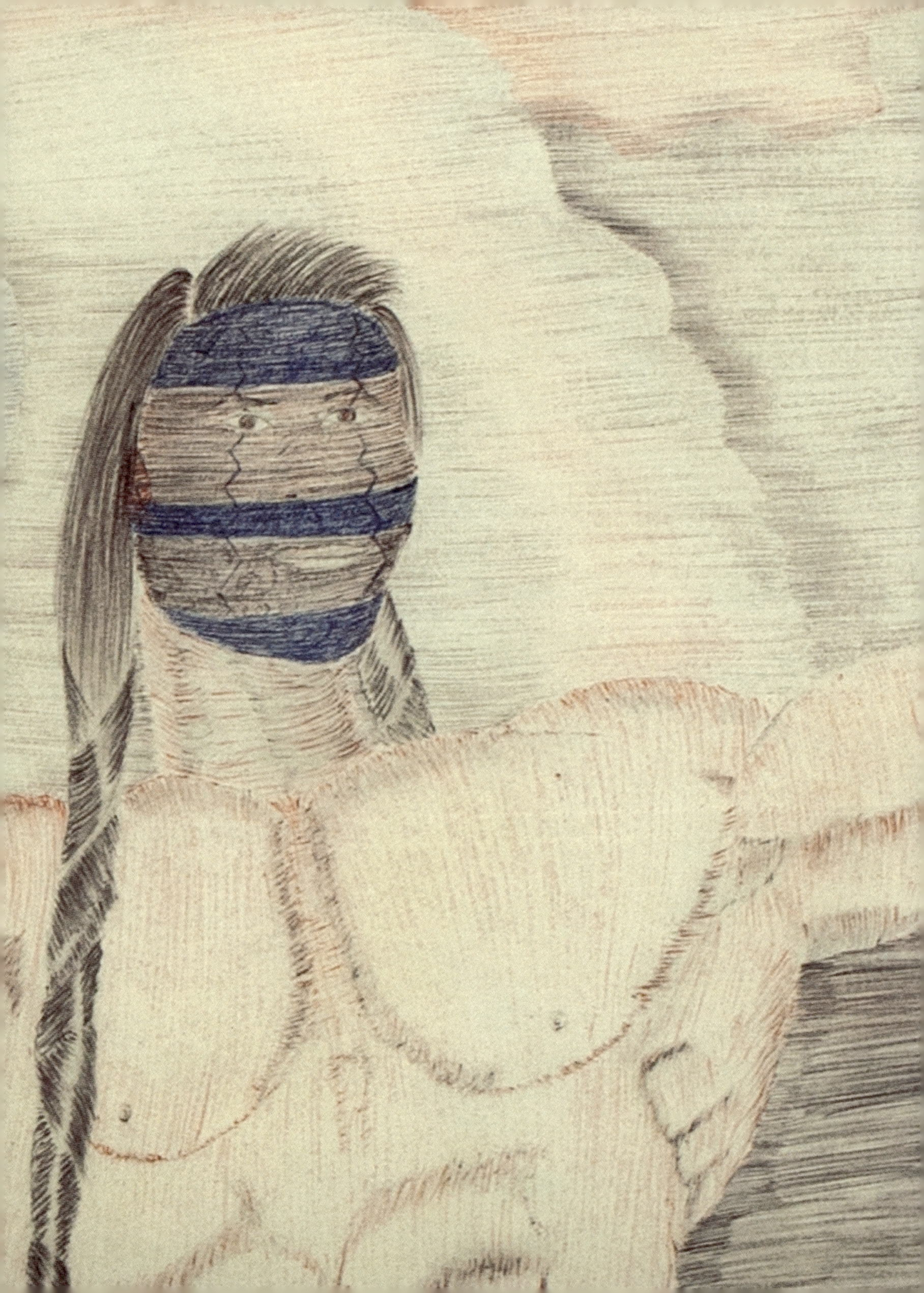

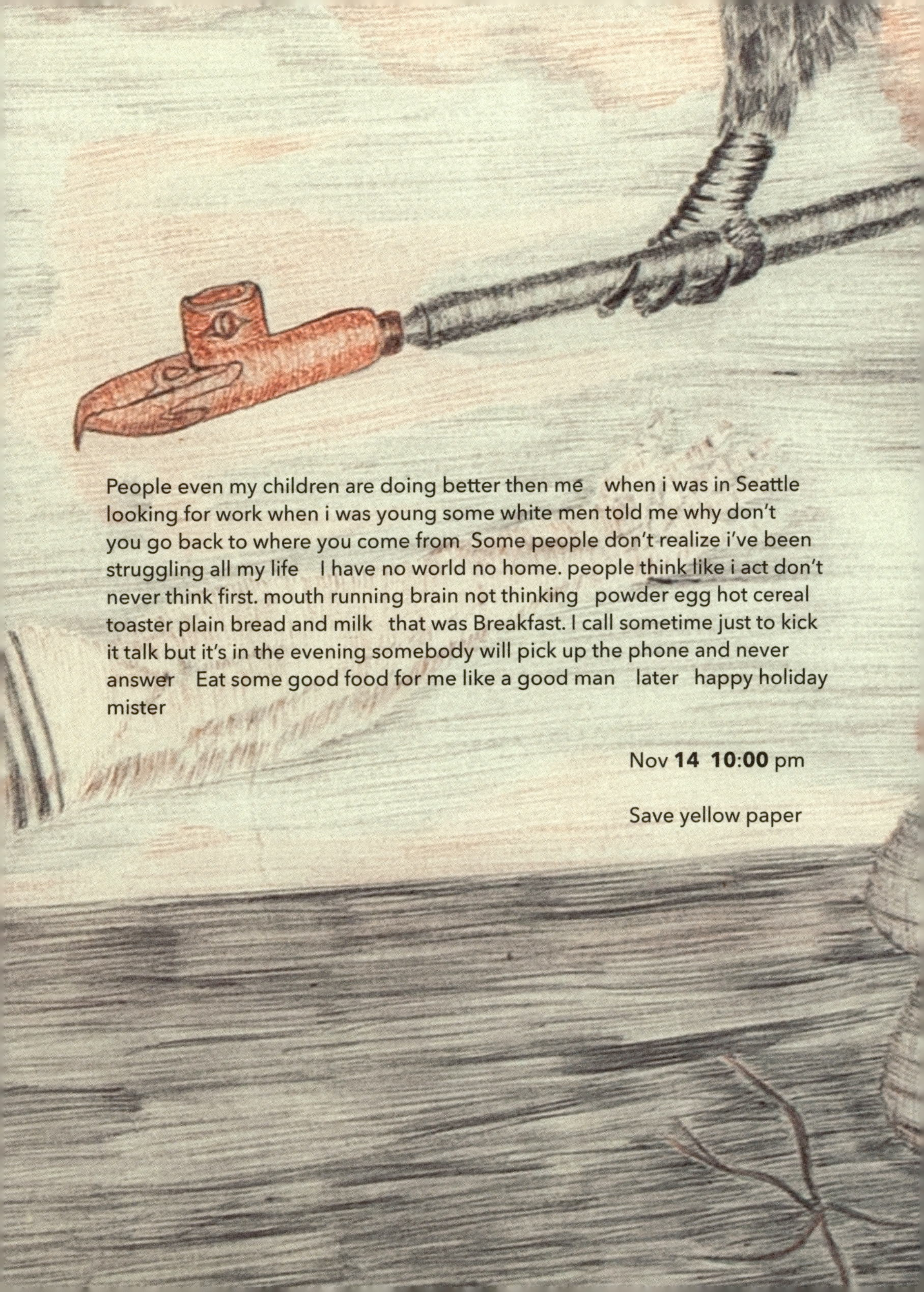

People even my children are doing better then me   when i was in Seattle
looking for work when i was young some white men told me why don't
you go back to where you come from Some people don't realize i've been
struggling all my life   I have no world no home. people think like i act don't
never think first. mouth running brain not thinking   powder egg hot cereal
toaster plain bread and milk   that was Breakfast. I call sometime just to kick
it talk but it's in the evening somebody will pick up the phone and never
answer   Eat some good food for me like a good man   later   happy holiday
mister

Nov **14 10:00** pm

Save yellow paper

The west is a singular mélange of rodeos, carnivals, county fairs, freak shows, gold mines, and a slew of whimsical roadside attractions. Entertainment aside, it is the desert that beckons. Vast, wide-open spaces that go on forever are punctuated by jutting rocks looking like they've been going somewhere for an eternity. The highway's dotted white line keeps your eyes pinned as you drive 130 miles-an-hour and it feels like you're doing 20. Cacti float by looking like a series of minimal parallax dances in an eerie aura of slow-motion. The "wild west" was indeed a productive centrifuge for Hollywood: Gunsmoke, Have Gun Will Travel, Rawhide, Bonanza, Zorro, Wagon Train, Stagecoach and so many more. Native Americans characters were always present and heavily stereotyped.

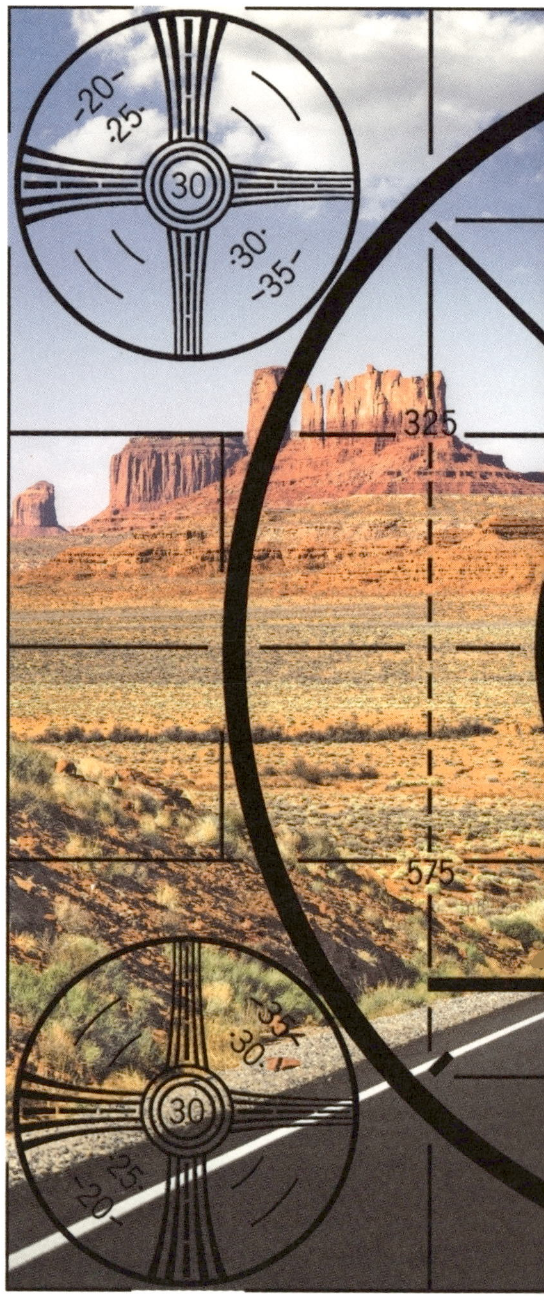

RCA Indian-head test pattern over image of route 163, Monument Valley, Arizona
Photo: Sean Pavone

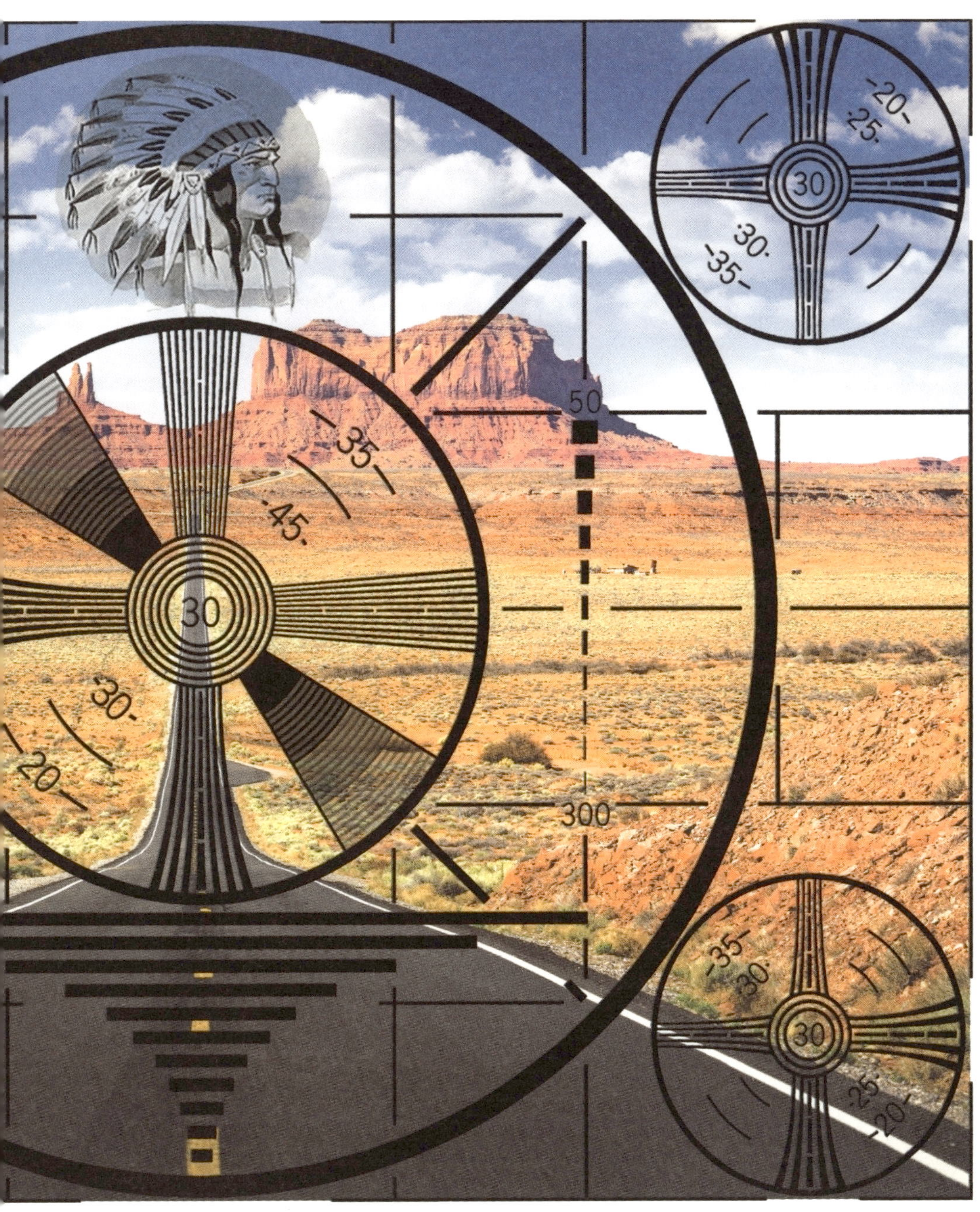
-20-
-25-
30
30-
-35-
50
-35-
-45-
30
-30-
-20-
300
-35-
-30-
30
-25-
-20-

Gary

Hi How's it going   good   **4**th July you + your family have   be safe. Hope this lette find's you and your family well. Thank you very much for takeing care of the tapes. i relly do appricate that   thank you from the bottom of my life. One punk say's he did not get his tape   The tape is made by Lynette   yes or no   will call. So did you enjoy your surfing   i hope so   how's your women   I hope fine. I'am just trying to keep my mind busy in this small world. I'am start computer class in july   going to go to school   Something diffrent   Just thinking about my dad alot   never thought i would think about him like i'am everyday in fact. Yes iam studing your picture you want i just having it on the boad in looking trying to get the feel for it. Thank you for the cash gary. Somehow i will get it back to you. Plus thank's for saying to me and a frind to you + a tiny family way   feels good   here's recipt what i pay on bead's. It cold in here tonight. God i want out   tird of this place   want freedom   i no   wha! cry! cry! Ha

I was drawing a pictur n i had it stuck on my wall   they gave me a warning take it down or get a write up   screw up

        Later Gary
          Peace

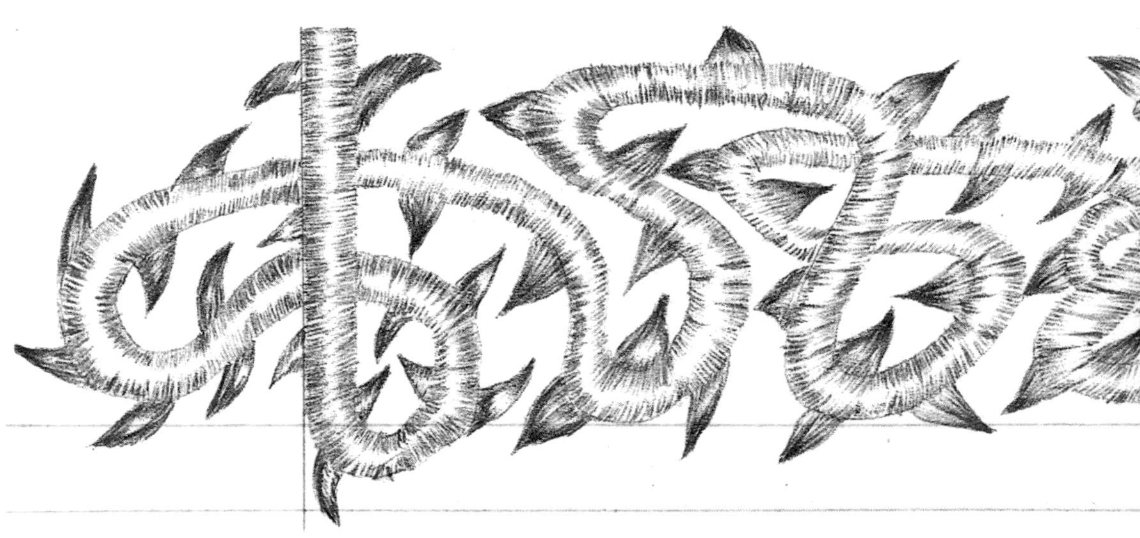

Well you kno I'll need a few dollars from you when you get back so send money if you can **35**% killing my accounts   It starting to get cold here below **0**   they say they turn heater on then they turn it off cruel basterd either it to hot or cold   borrow a sweatshirt from somebody sleep with my sweats on or pants plus my hat crazy huh   Fri - **3-000 8:30** pm told to lock down   **4** native bro beat down 3 guards behind the wall   one is in a coma   One Guard talk to me about it, I told them we want NO trouble   pretty crazy in here at times just came in from the yard the chaplain n leautient here threaten to write me up for calling the chaplain prejudice racist they say it's threatening the men ha! ha! their moveing me again to another prison   I don't kno when Happy Thanksgiving   I bought a couple turtles in a little leather box so when he's done he will send them or when you send the money there. I should have a couple checks there by the time you get back   It's raining here in getting cold. Who is the next president   Can't even spell unless i have a dictionairy
      I worte this letter a long time ago still here will send letter when they ship me

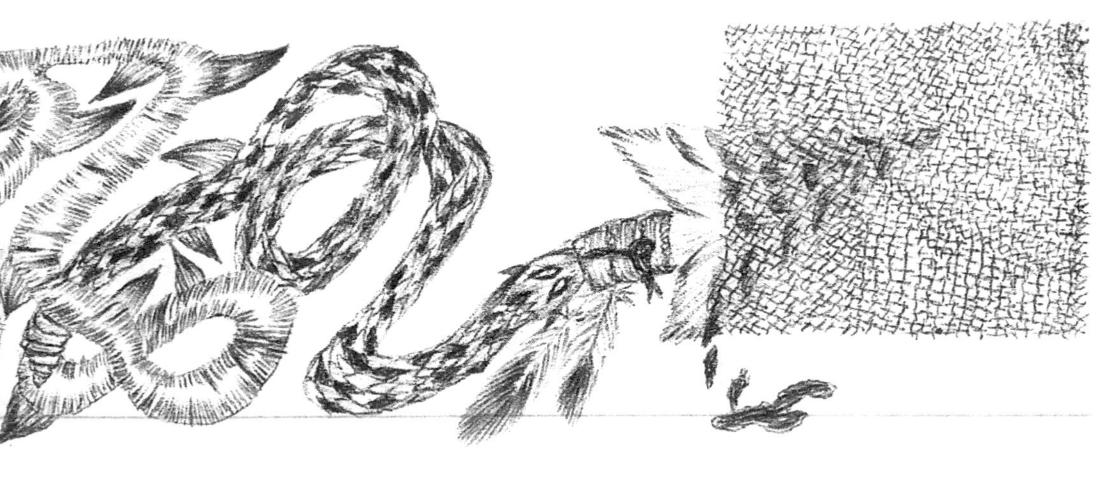

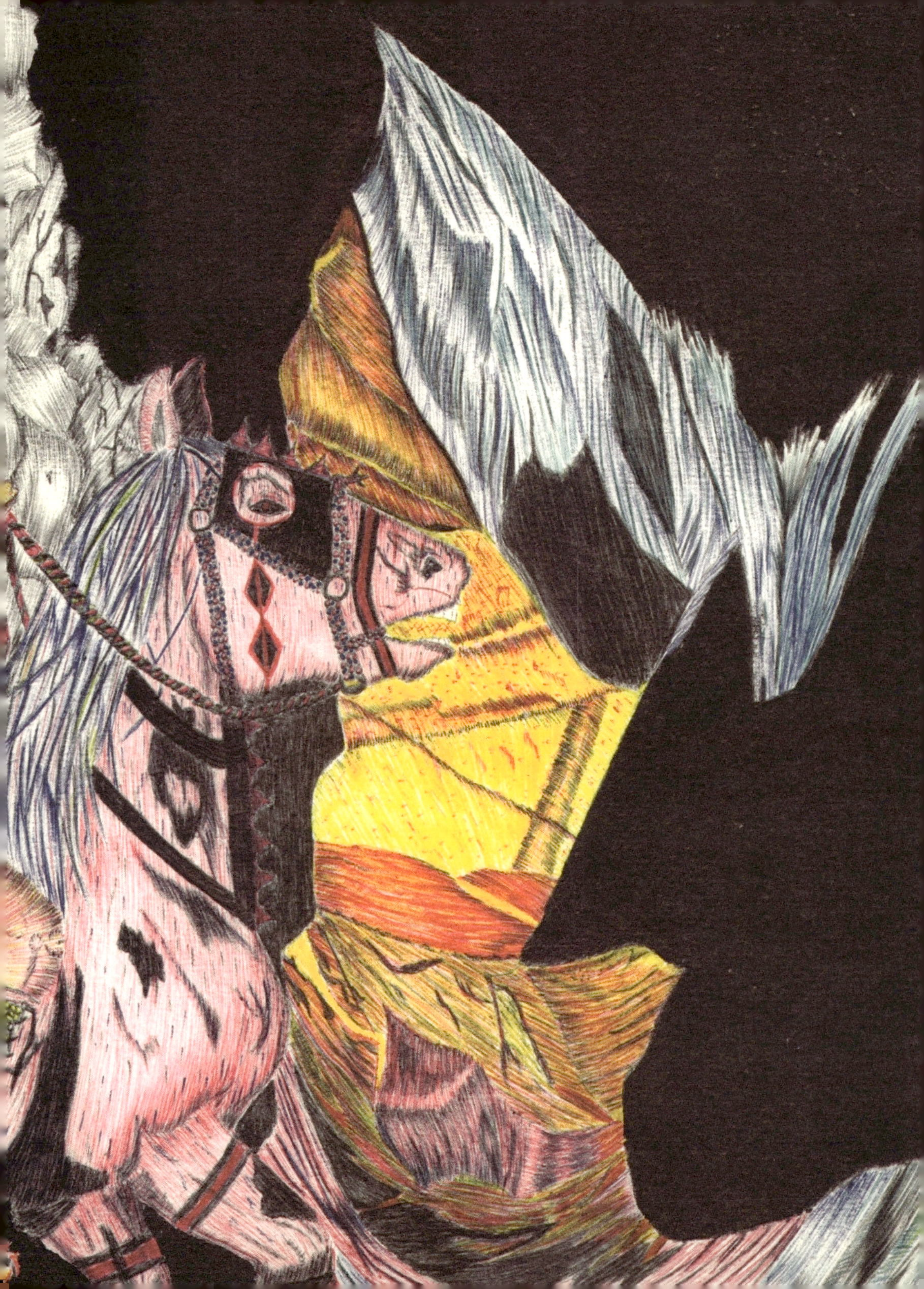

INFORMATION UPDATE REGARDING
CROWLEY COUNTY CORRECTIONS FACILITY

An inmate disturbance at the Crowley County Corrections Facility began in the yard at approximately 7:30 p.m. on Tuesday evening, July 20th. Colorado Department of Corrections Emergency Response and Special Operations Response Teams were brought in and subsequently quelled the active disturbance. It is our understanding that the inmates involved are from all jurisdictions.

As of 8:00 a.m., 500 inmates were being contained in an outdoor area. There were 12 inmates reportedly injured; 4 of which came from Washington. Two Washington inmates suffered gunshot (pellet) wounds which are not life threatening.

Some news accounts have identify Washington inmates as the instigators. However, this information has not been confirmed by any official source. Be mindful that rumors often run rampant when these types of situations occur.

Washington Department of Corrections staff have arrived at Crowley and will be doing an initial assessment of the situation. At this point, we do not anticipate inmates being returned to Washington except for those who require Intensive Management placement.

Joe Ortiz, Executive Director for the Colorado Department of Corrections said, "We will thoroughly investigate the incident and the inmate leaders will be referred for prosecution."

Lori Scamahorn
Public Information/Legal Liaison Officer
Washington State Penitentiary

Fast-forward forty years, it's 1996
and I'm in the midst of videotaping
('shooting' as filmmakers like to say)
strangers—day laborers that happen
to get their working papers and a meal
now and then just across the street from
where I live. Living one day to the next,
men line up outside a social service
facility called "The Millionaires Club."
For the most part they are Mexicans,
ostensibly "illegal" but nobody much
cared then. Among them there was a
scattering of blacks along with a few
Native Americans in the predominantly
white city of Seattle.

I'm working on an installation that
would become *Viewer*. Approximately
life-size color images of seventeen
day-laborers, facing out from a neutral
dark background, are projected
on a single wall. The figures stand
almost motionless, their movement
limited to involuntary stirring—an
incidental shuffling from foot to foot,
slight movements of the hands and
almost imperceptible changes in facial
expressions. There is no interaction
among them, each man standing quite
alone and gazing out from the plane of
projection towards the viewer.

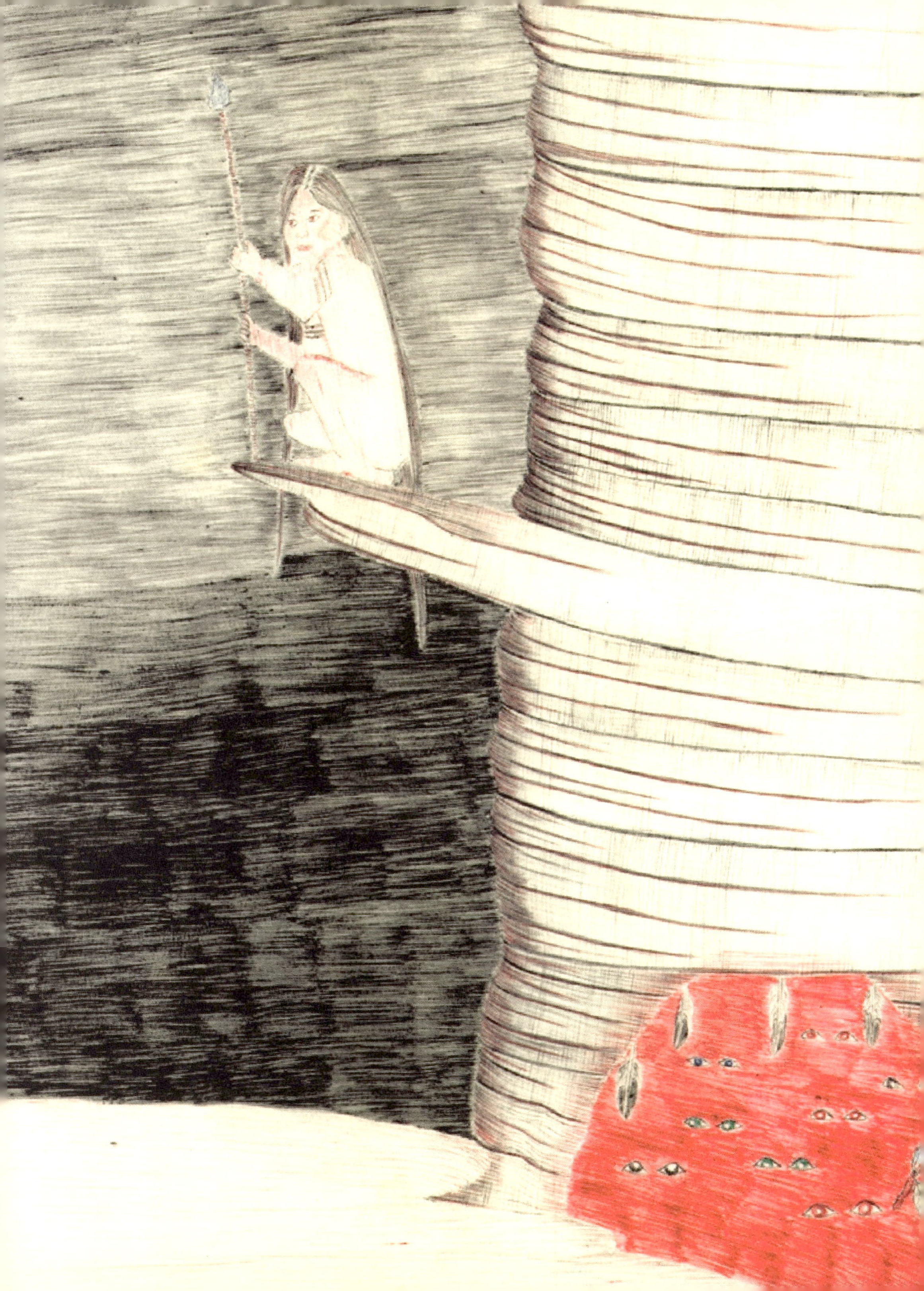

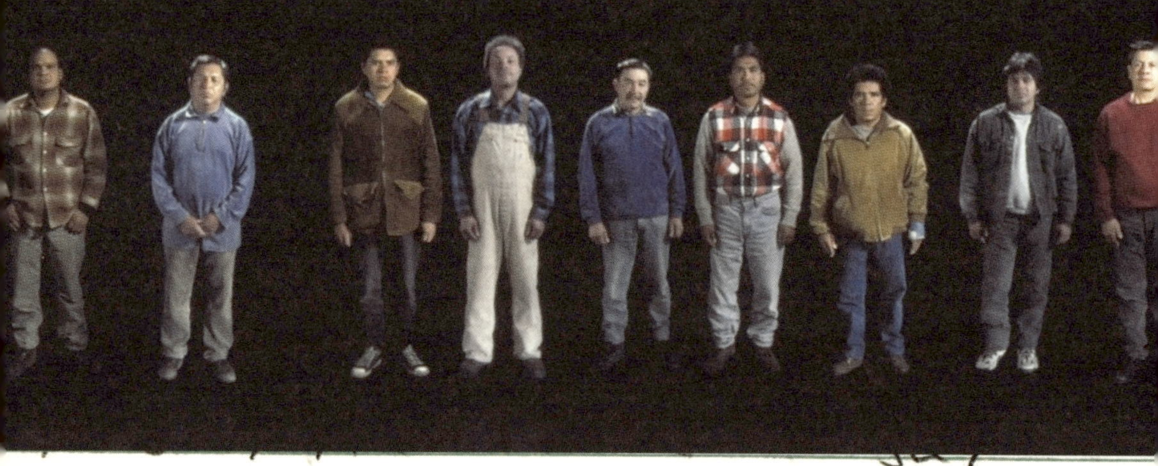

comeing up   i get to
up in down this cage in
beauti7ol
Hour. Sn
Penitentiary

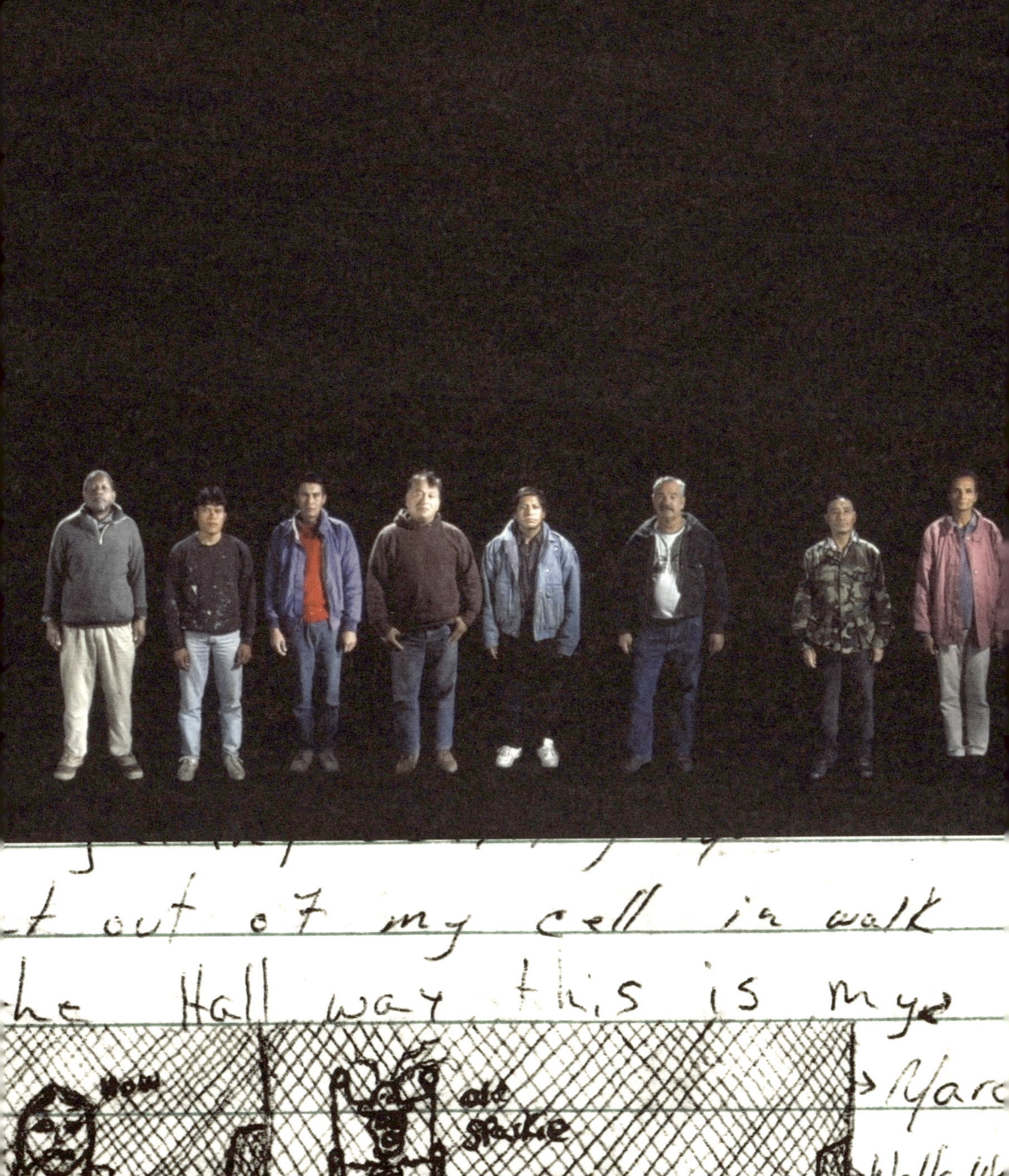
t out of my cell in walk
he Hall way this is my
Now
old
Spikie
→Mar
→Walla Wa
→Pris

The first time I caught a glimpse of Martin he was crossing Western Ave heading for the Millionaires Club. His six-foot-plus stature stood out along with his angular sculpted face framed by two long braids of raven black hair. He was wearing tennis shoes and a jean jacket. Agile and quick on his feet, Martin was a dead ringer for a "warrior" outside of space and time. Yet his complexity always resisted any kind of closure having to do with defining said Native American. He seemed to want to shed the image of the res and define his individuality in a multiplicity of ways, nevertheless he always projected a deep respect for his roots and what the revered elders had passed down. By the sheer will on his face he could've been the brother of Chief Bromden, the unforgettable Indian in One Flew Over the Cuckoo's Nest. Seems like all Indians fly over the cuckoo's nest one way or another. How shocking to discover that there were more Native American soldiers per capita than any other ethnicity that fought in the Vietnam War—"the horror, the horror..."

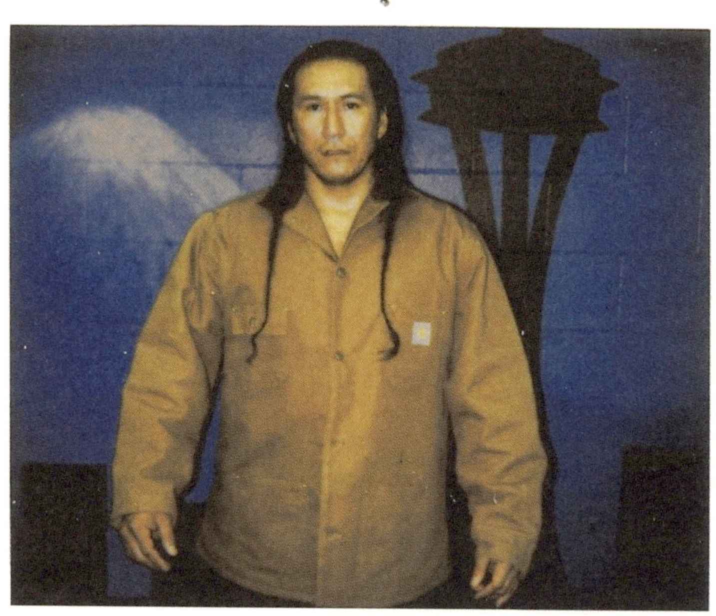

Good Mourning World Tues. **16** Nov.
My third World of being lock uup   I'am just rembering walking down the
water front with a pretty young lady doing pharmacal speed drinking beer
and haveing a good time haveing hot sex yes it was a beautiful evening and
mourning enjoy all night   **17** Nov mourning went to a meeting to see if i
was eligabul to go to a out of state transfer to Colorado Colado Colorado
don't no how to spell it   they say it crowded here   But right now they say no
so that good with me. KNowing my luck the plane would crash and i would
go down like Huey Lewis down in a ball of flames   Went outside n it was
cold out < So how are you today? have you relly ask yourself that or look
at yourself you probly thinking I'am not locked up so I'm doing better then
you, yes i would imagine   so today is the **21**th Nov we've been lockdown 1
nite 1 day for a fight or stabbing don't relly no been inside this unit for two
week left it **4** times only waiting for dinner right now   Today is the **25**th of
November It's Raining out. The nite before Thanksgiving waiting to go to
my prison yard n match them play Basketball looking at a magazin with a
Beautiful Blond on The Cover thinking about those California girls   i work
there for two yr. **1/4** cup fresh lime juice cucmbir **2** tablespoons brown sugar
2 table spoons vegetable oil **1** tablespoon Worcestershire sauce **3** large
cloves garlic crushed **1** beef top round steak about **1** lb marinat for **6** hours
145° F turning occasionally **10-11** minute **6-9** min on grill   Today is the **26**
Nov Black Friday **11:35** AM the year of **2000**   No matter how hard i clean this
room it still stinks of baddness like a old time urinal nasty.   sometimes the
hold building smell like that

Opposite page: Martin Cothren
Monroe Correctional Complex

I doubt if Martin ever had to contend with the possibility of military service. What would be my brief encounter with Uncle Sam petrified me and reared its ugly head the morning that the draft lottery numbers were posted:

Along with a friend in the same boat, we headed down to the Woodstock general store to find out what fate had dealt. He was number 285 and a very happy soul. My number? 37. I got a letter within two weeks to report to the draft board. I knew this was coming but I had planned for it well before the lottery system was enacted. Back in high school, I had already started to build a psychological case that hopefully would support the idea that I wasn't fit for the army. I started to see a psychologist and week after week spun tales of obsession, feelings of despair, and being utterly asocial. Much of it I slowly convinced myself was partially true. I vaguely remember the school IQ test and being literally off the chart in the column measuring social interaction. I was asked to draw a picture of a person. I drew a crucifixion with weird intricate patterns all over the page. I sent stream of consciousness letters and meaningless objects to the draft board having heard they had to file and keep anything and everything they received.

I had a plan and the most important part of that plan was simply to know down deep I wasn't goin'. Period. I didn't sleep for 3 days or bathe for a week before my scheduled time. That morning I took one hit of sunshine (LSD) and started hitchhiking to Kingston where we'd be picked up and bussed to Albany for processing. A strange professorial type in a Volkswagen bug gave me a lift. He looked like his car—large thick eyebrows with a matching mustache—now picture a frontal view of the bug. Not much different than how people resemble their dogs, sometimes uncannily so. This was of course more extreme having ingested my drug of choice. Arriving in Kingston, a kind of way station, I happened to be just peaking and the place was full of some very hard-core folk from the surrounding, somewhat depressed small towns. One fellow, wearing a poncho, stood upright in front of an electric fan letting the wind blow through his hair. He seemed to be talking to the device itself, at times, sounding as if he were speaking in tongues. Others grouped together with somber looks on their faces and not a whole lot to say. We finally boarded the bus for the hour and a half long journey. I was high as a kite and falsely felt 50 pairs of eyes studying my every movement. One guy comes up to the slovenly character next to me and starts talking tough about wimps getting doctor's notes for easy deferments. I think he was implying me but he was wrong. I wished I had a note saying I was schizophrenic, psychotic or whatever—anything. I thought, "what's wrong with this asshole;" he already sounded like a fucking marine. We arrived. My idea was to score as close to perfect as possible on all tests, and then utilize the available psychosis that the drug could generate. I was already starting to come down a bit as I was approaching the last cubicle. I thought, it's now or never... I saw a section of linoleum floor that was swirling with multiple colors and tapped into it to get me started. I threw myself on the floor ranting and raving about absolutely nothing, but the truncated episode managed to get me to the shrink who dismissed me with a 1Y and "we'll see you in 6 months."

By now I was fried and had no desire to wait for the bus and maintain myself amongst those who I now gathered were seasoned draft dodgers that had been doing this repeatedly. I headed down to the highway and from up on the overpass I saw the man with the poncho standing on the corner in search of a ride. He greeted my stare with a raised arm and opened hand. I had little choice but to join him. We walked a bit and he attempted speaking with what sounded like a serious speech impediment. We came to a point where we'd split and go our separate ways. As I crossed the street, he yelled out, "hey man, take it easy," in perfect English mind you. After he had assured himself I wasn't "the man," he waved and was on his way.

Meanwhile, it's pouring rain and I'm drenched, trying to get a ride. Finally, somebody pulls over and within minutes the fucker politely suggests we take the next exit and he'll suck me off. No thank you, drop me off here... now! I'm frazzled—I don't know who's what and where I'm going anymore. I see a bus coming down the highway and I'm sure it's the same bus; I run into the trees to hide (as if it would stop anyway). The last thing in the world I wanted to do was get back on that bus. Sooner or later a big ol' white Cadillac Eldorado stops. It's a lone driver dressed in a white suit and a cowboy hat, smoking a cigar. I got a good vibe and, given my state of mind, I felt I had nothing to lose. The radio was playing—can't remember what it was—and the car was warm and comforting. He turned out to be a kind southerner on his way to Saugerties. Seeing that I was clearly in a bad state, he went out of his way and took me all the way to my door—a side entrance to a basement hovel where I lived and made sculpture at the time.

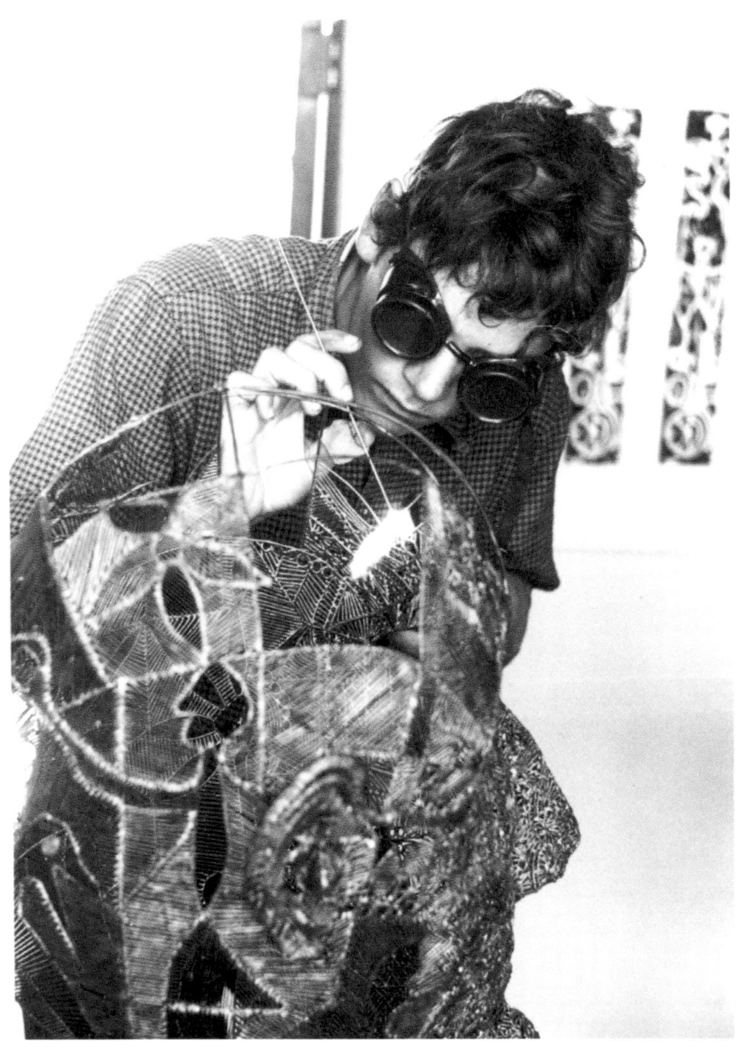

Gary Hill, Redondo Beach studio, 1968
photo: Mark White

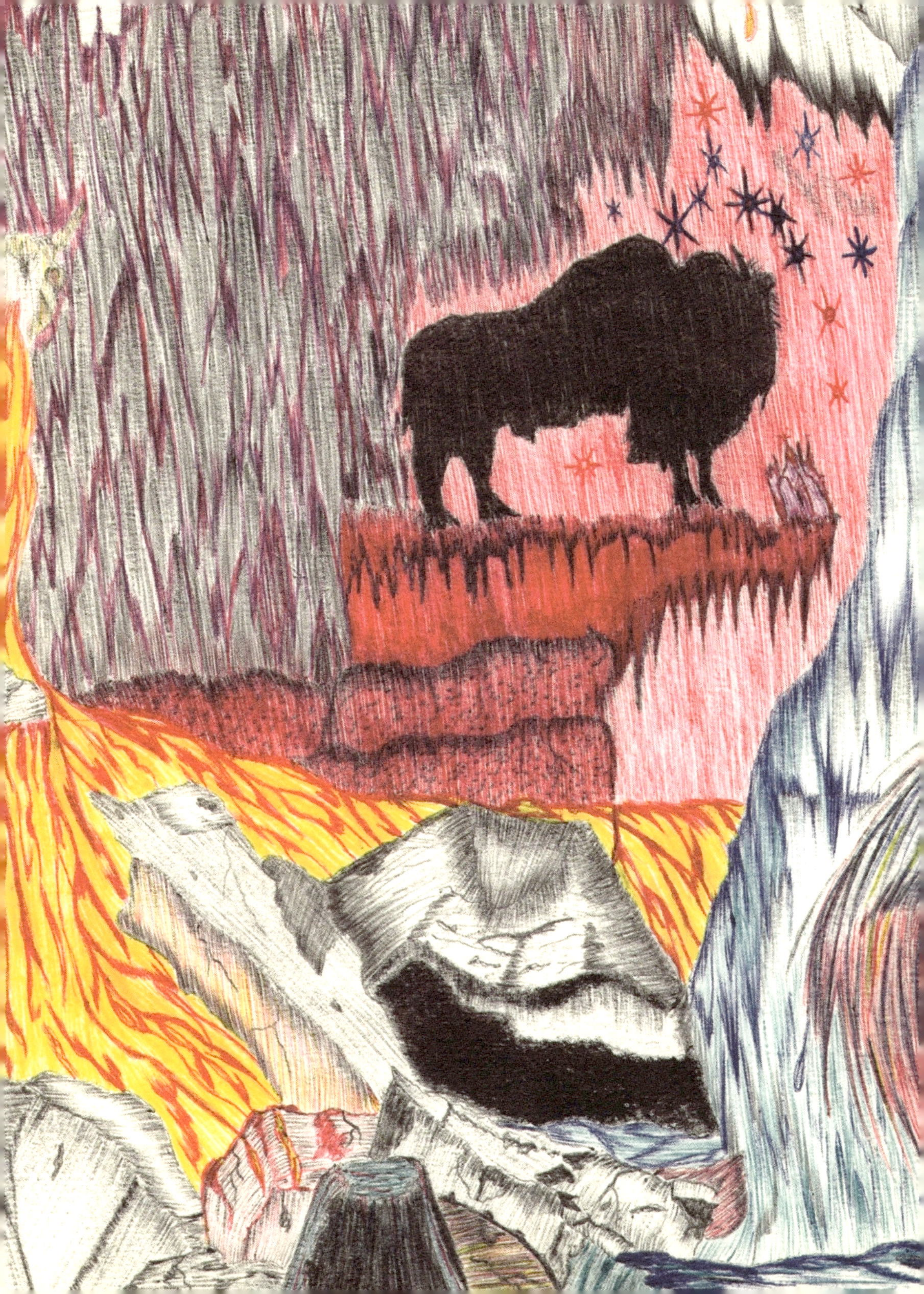

"Hi, are you looking for work?"

"Maybe, what's up?"

"Well, something a little different than maybe what you're used to. I'm an artist and live just across the street; I'm recording people around here that are looking for work, one at a time. All you have to do is stand across from me while we take each other in--something like maintaining an energy between us, a kind of communion..."
"An artist huh...alright, let's check it out. I'm not so into having my picture taken."

I could tell he was uncomfortable but I wasn't sure if it boiled down to shyness or something about the politics of one's image that he'd already briefly mentioned.

Nevertheless, it didn't take long for Martin to grasp the nature of the project. He was into it, though his imposing presence made me nervous at times. Most others did the least they could do wanting to get out of there as fast as possible with a few bucks. Martin was unique; he had a kind of quiet intelligence different from the others, so much so he inspired another work—*Facing Faces*. Certainly related, but rather than being about purely present energy, it focused on a singular action, exchanging focused attention with one's doppelganger and the viewer with the idea to dynamically triangulate the three into the space of the gaze.

Opposite page: Indian Head nickel
Designed by sculptor, James Earle Fraser

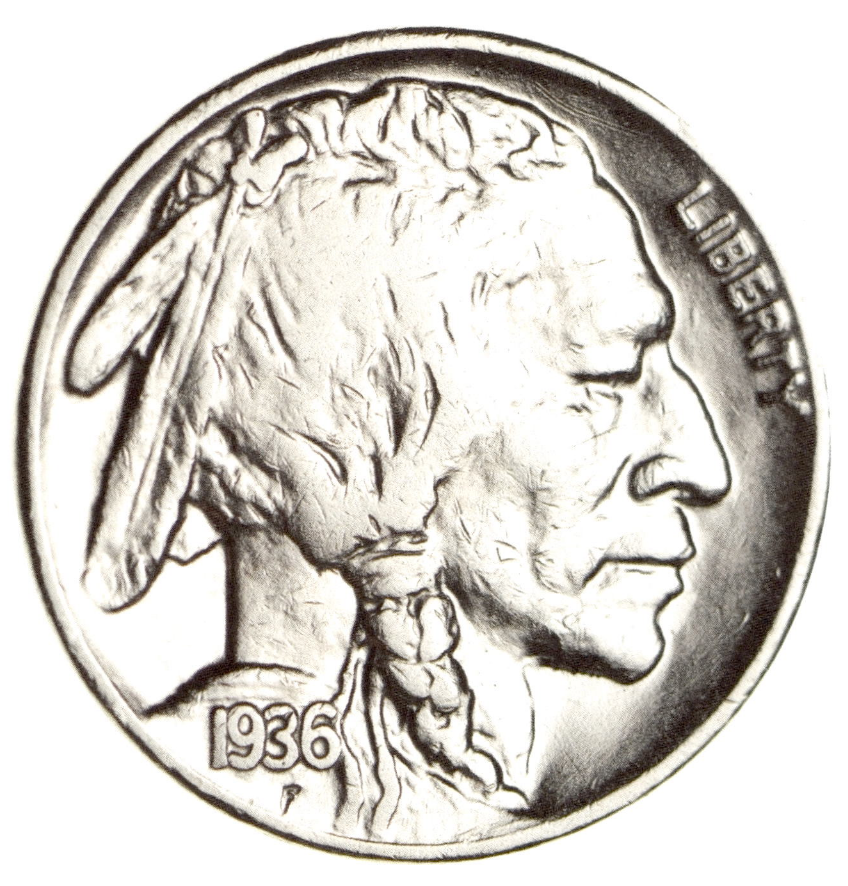

"*How do you like to be called— Native American, First Nation, Yakama, American Indian, or something else?*"

"*I'm an Indian. The rest are just word games.*"

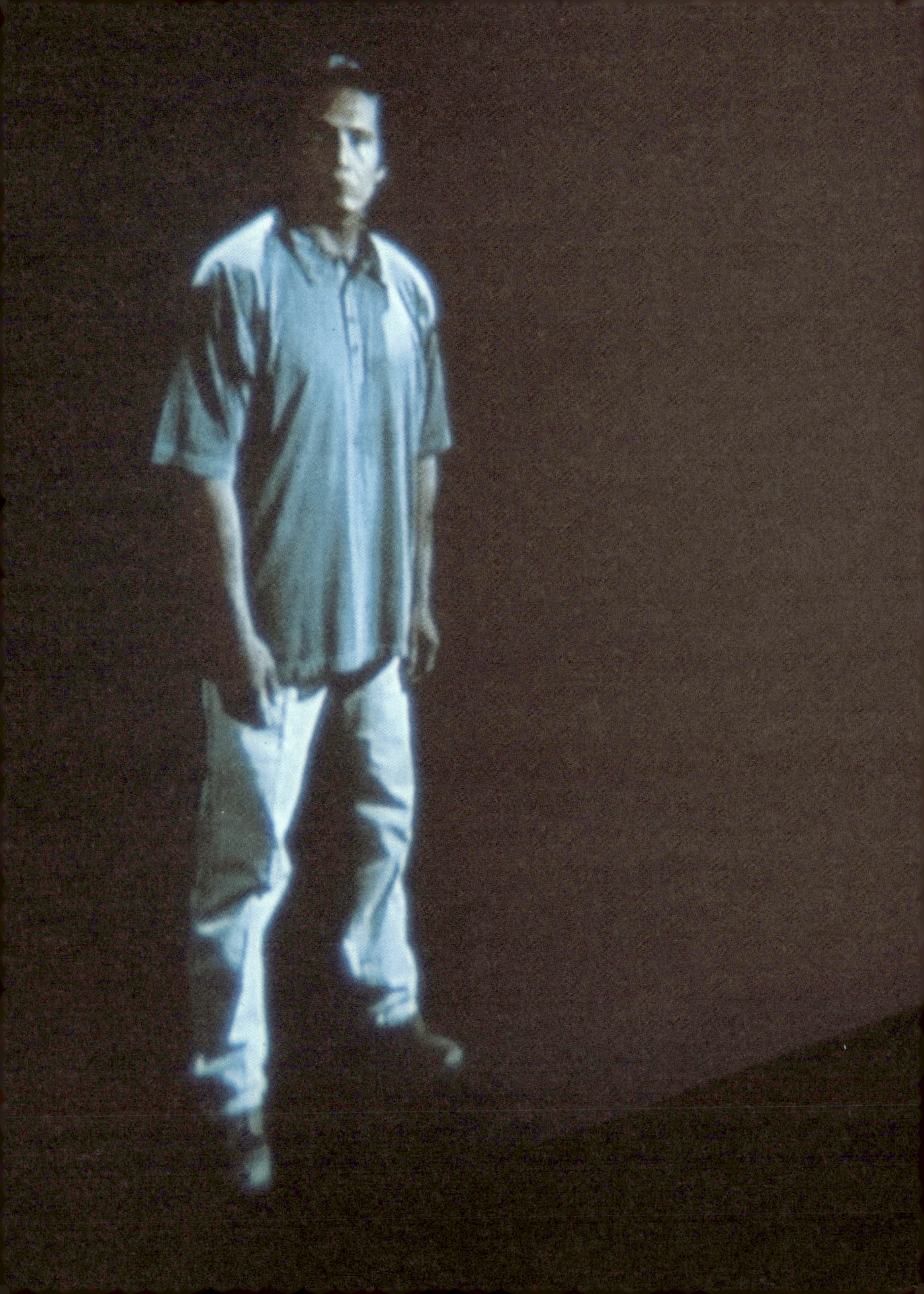

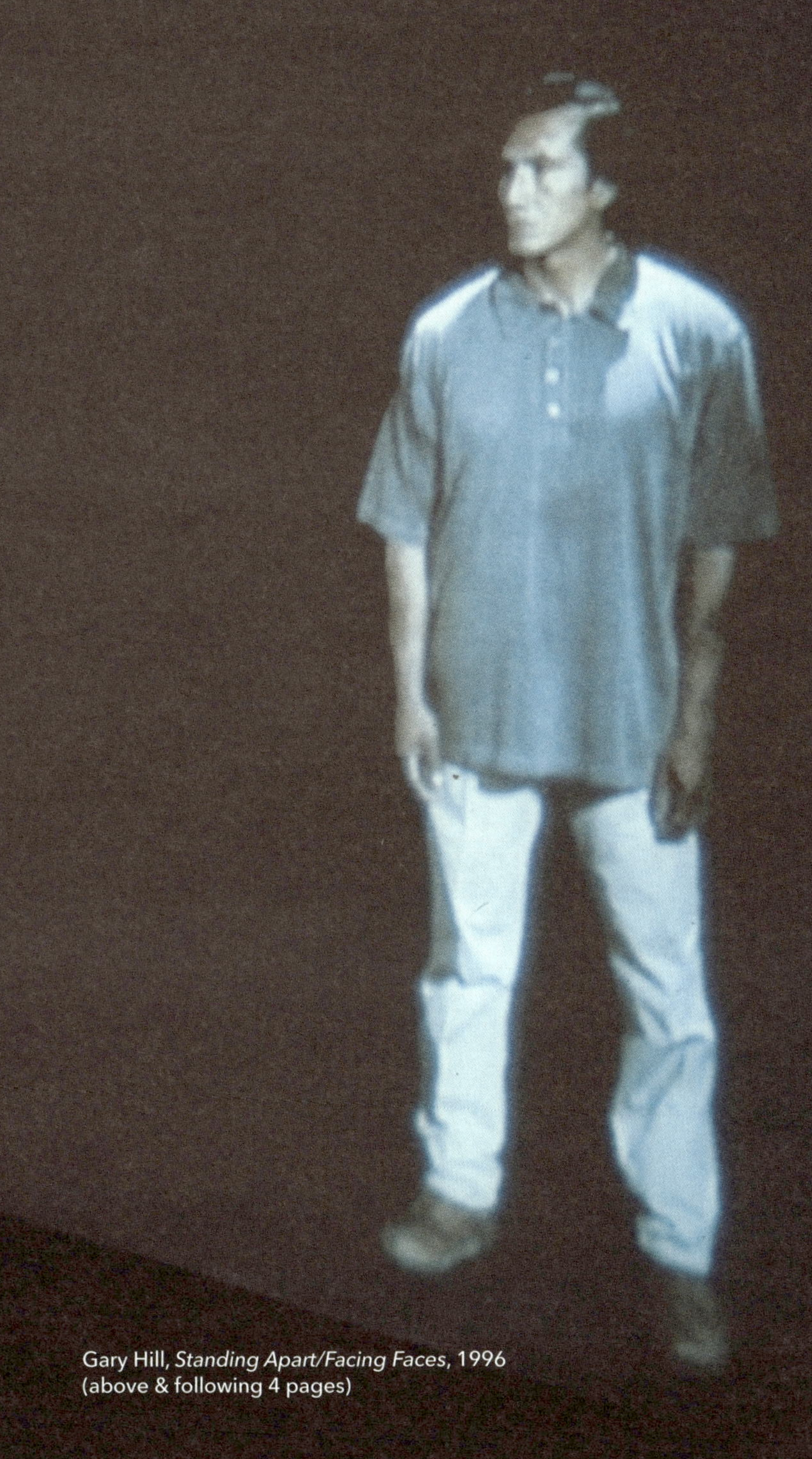

Gary Hill, *Standing Apart/Facing Faces*, 1996
(above & following 4 pages)

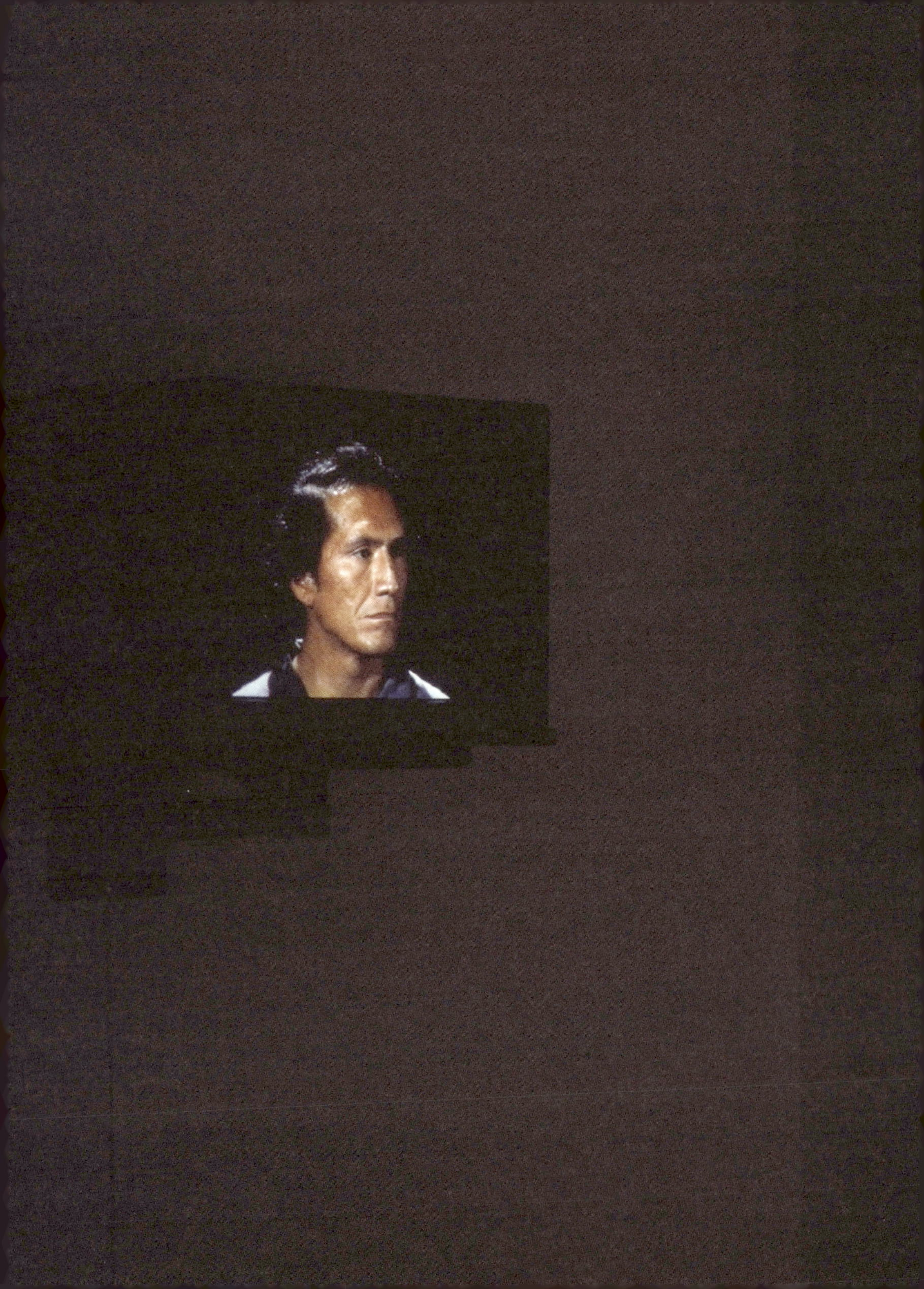

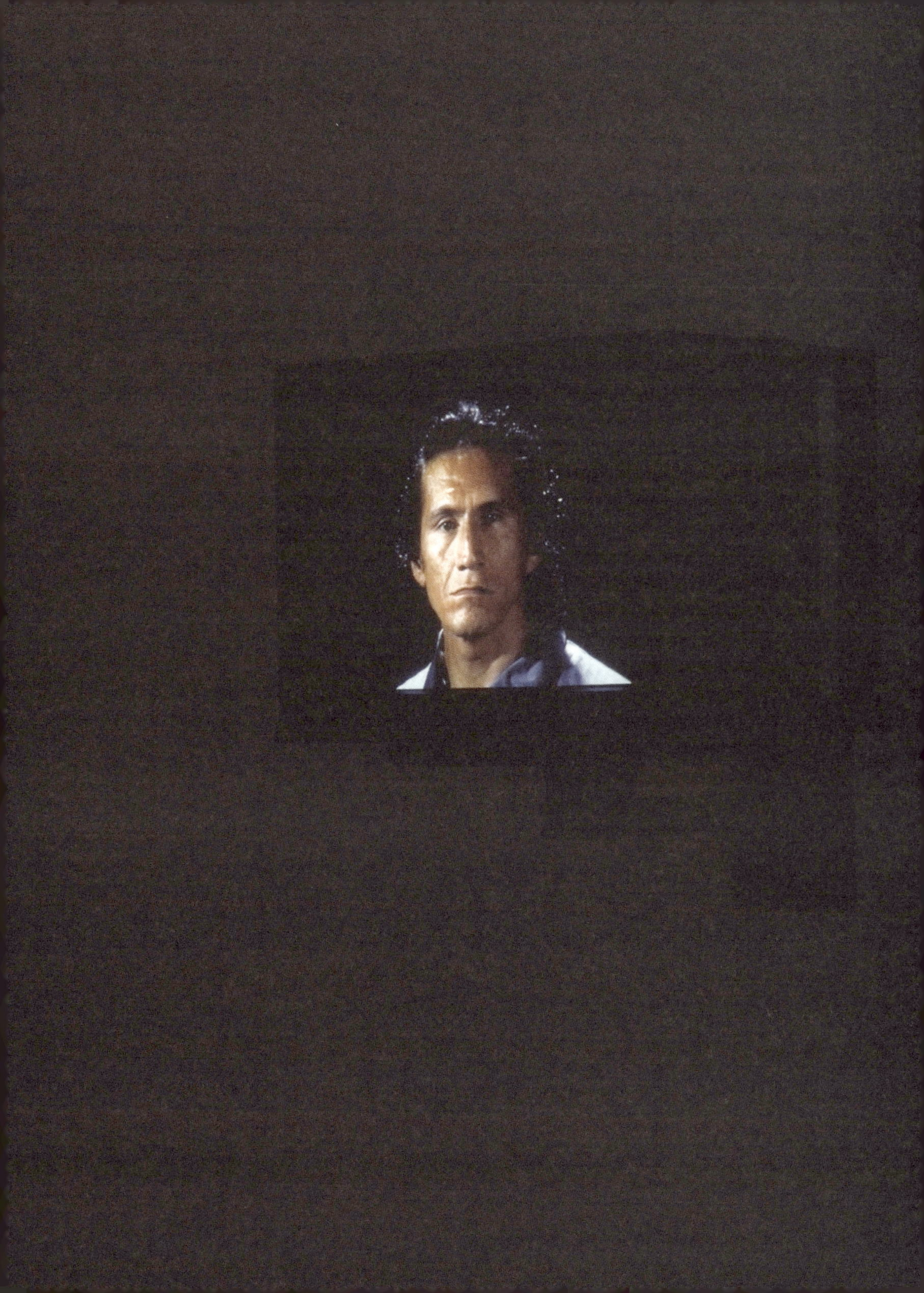

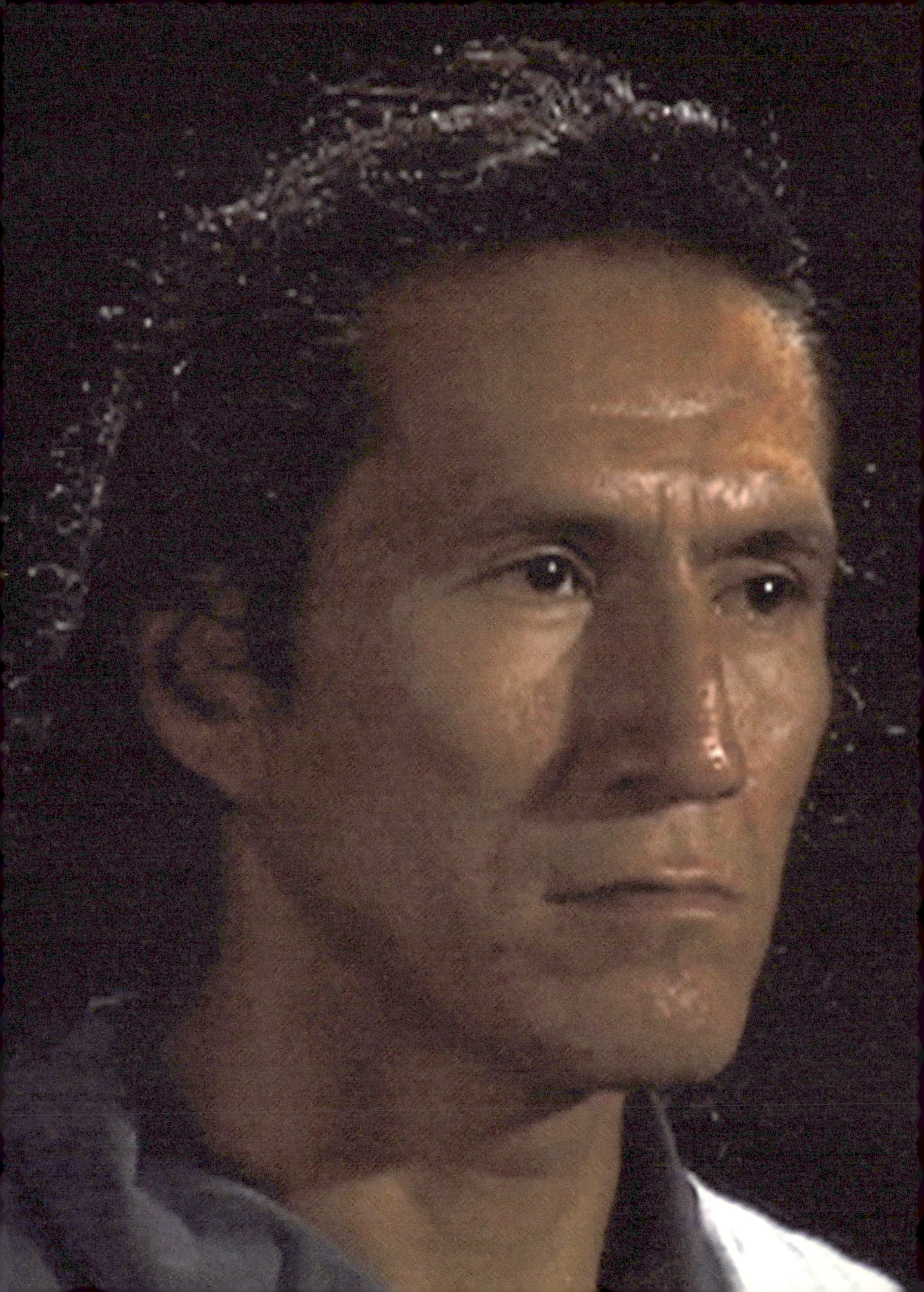

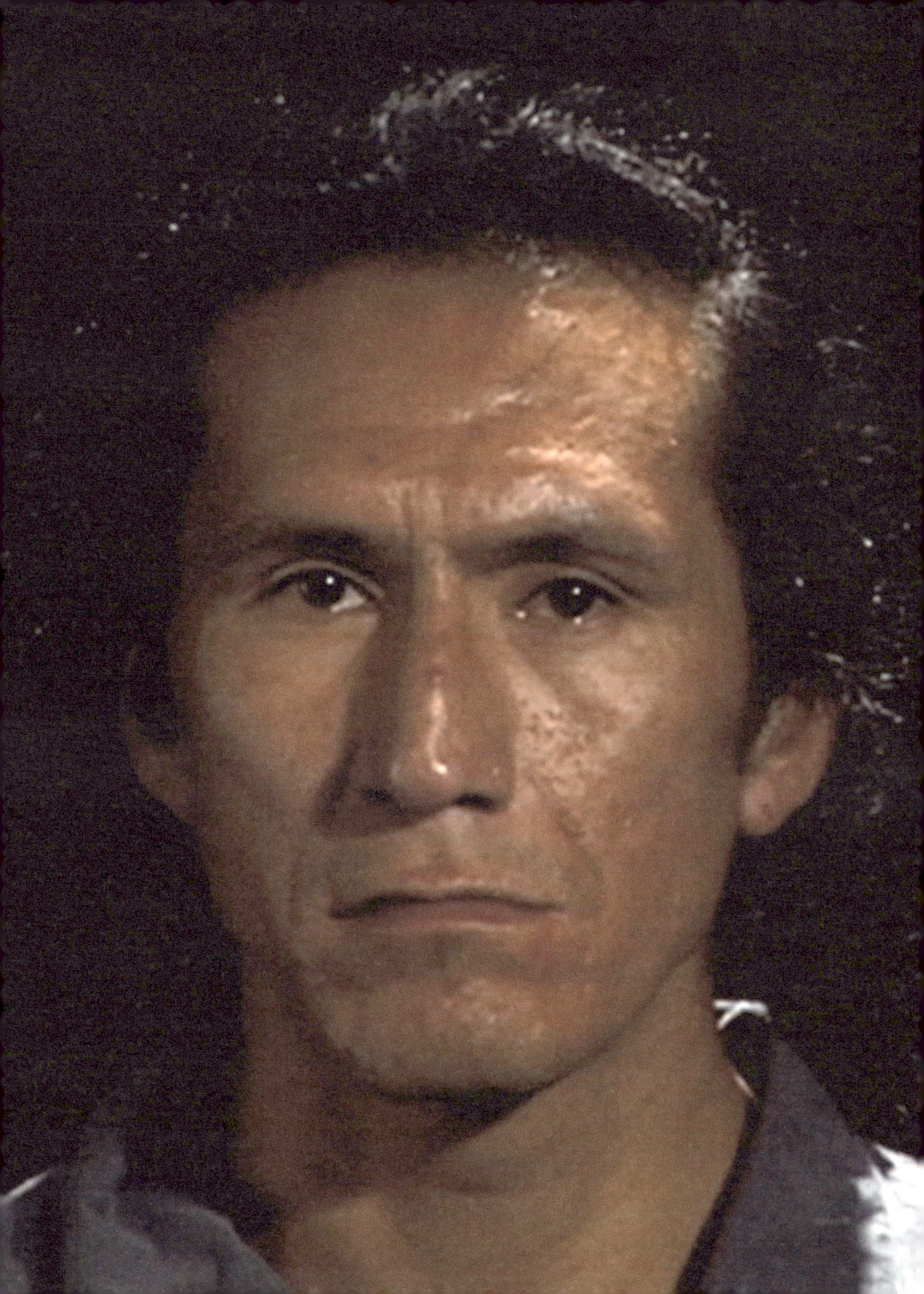

I paid him for his work and we went for a drink. This was my first mistake of many to come. I knew it was a bad idea and thought to quickly change plans but my legs kept their gait and soon we were throwing back a few.

A similar sort of bifurcation happened long ago and has stayed gnarled up in my psyche ever since:

Hitchhiking home after a late-night chess club had dispersed, a station wagon with four bad boys maybe a year or two younger than my 19 years stopped to give me a lift. Two in the front, two in the back. One punk got out and offered me ingress. Once again, I couldn't overcome the body/mind cleave (why would he get out of the car to have me sit in the middle?) Moot point now. I was sitting between two twerps as I scoped out the scene and uttered in my mind a long slow f u c k …Away we went and that's when all the fun began. I tried to be light-hearted even ironic informing them about how far down the road I'd be disembarking. The evident "leader," riding shotgun, was visibly fucked up playing with a sizable switchblade as he traded barbs with his minions. Soon they were speaking of Clockwork Orange, cutting ears off and what not, all the while laughing hysterically and painfully loud. By now the tough one was leaning over the front seat and running the blade over my legs. As we passed my destination, my anxiety began morphing to serious fear. Soon we were on a dirt road in the middle of nowhere. The car stopped and the lights went off. Briefly, I thought to grab the knife and stick it to one of them next to me. Instead I was frozen— my abdomen waiting for the blade. Nothing I could do now. I offered what little money I had and suddenly the atmosphere changed. Were they just fucking with me? I'll never know. They took my beer money and started driving elsewhere…but I'm still their captive. Stopping again they pulled me out of the car; I made a run for it. The chase was short-lived, I was fast back in the day. Eventually I reached the main artery, out of breath and overcome with nausea. I stopped at a few houses pounding on the doors—nobody. Fortunately, I realized the big old pale-yellow Chevy station wagon had turned the other way. It was four in the morning by the time I stumbled upon my doorstep.

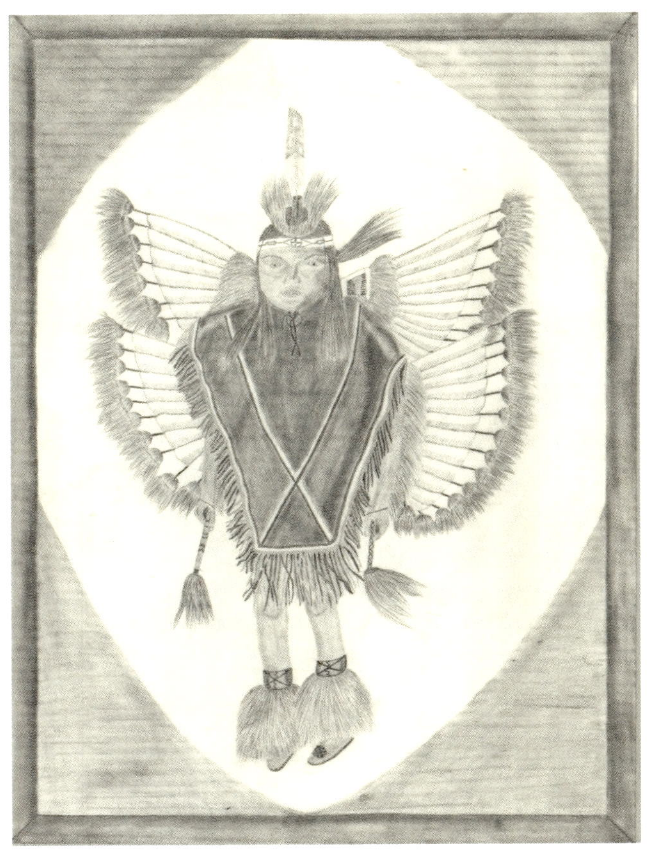

Back to the bar... a young woman joined us, taking a seat next to Martin. I presumed they had some kind of relationship. She was belligerent and rude, seemingly angry that her mate was having a cordial exchange with a white man. Martin was politely apologetic and calmed her down. As we exchanged quiet words around the use of his image, I came to know he was an avid drawer—ink and pencil for the most part but the surprise was he had been in a few films and at times wearing full Native regalia. In that regard, perhaps he saw this situation as a way to project himself in opposition to some cliché imposed upon him by the Hollywood industry. Maybe his aversion to being photographed had a caveat. I didn't question it as he didn't seem like the lying type—on the contrary, his word was his cornerstone. In hindsight there was no turning back from what would become an unlikely bond. It would be the beginning of a twenty year long odyssey.

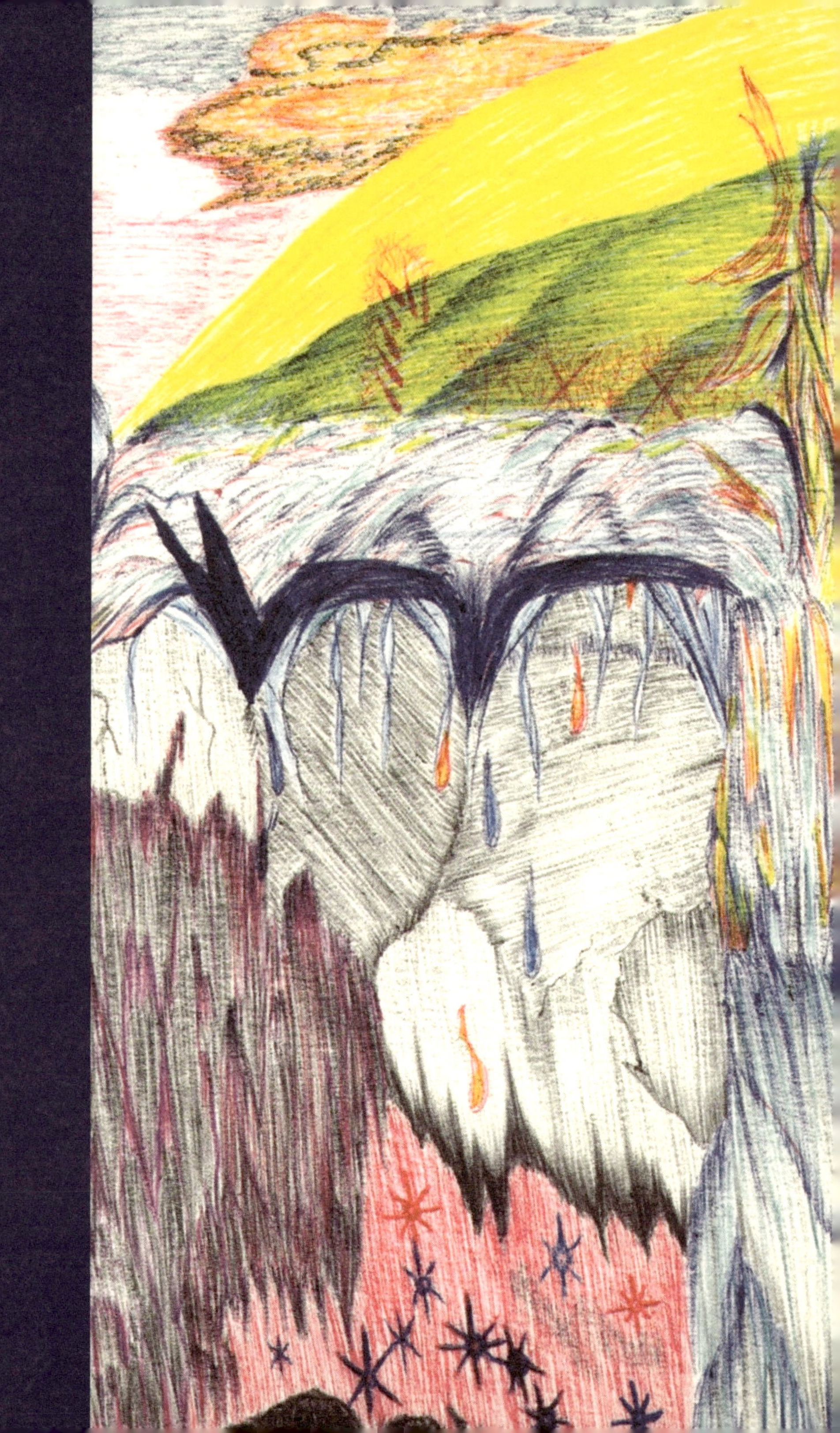

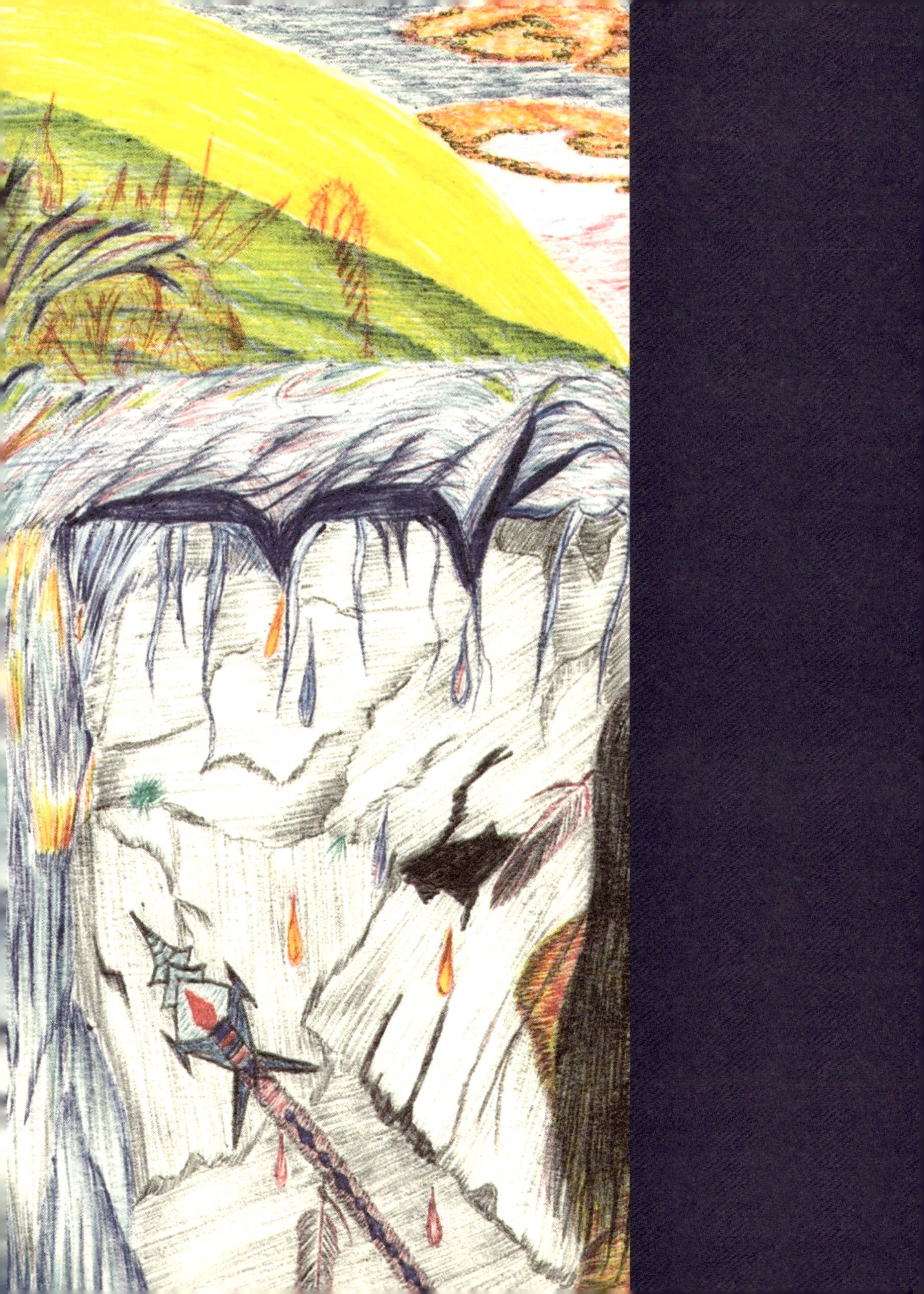

During the following weeks, Martin would come by now and then asking for a few bucks; we got together for coffee a couple of times and then on January 1, 1997 I got a call from the county jail. "Can you help me?"

They charged him with a felony. I hired an attorney to check it out—bad news—Washington State had recently implemented the three-strike policy—three felonies and one is automatically sentenced to life without parole. This was meant to deter "career criminals."

The state explained their reasoning with harsh examples, I will spare you with just one: "Reading the horror script of one of the first to be sentenced under Three Strikes would make anyone shutter. Strike One, second-degree rape in Montana, the monster dragged a 14-year-old girl into the woods and raped her. He was released after only a few weeks and followed up with Strike Two—attempted second-degree rape of a 15-year-old girl during a burglary. His Strike Three, again barely out for a month, he cut his wife's face and neck, rammed a 9-inch-bladed knife into her mouth, pointed a pellet gun at her head and told her that he 'would kill her anytime' he wished."

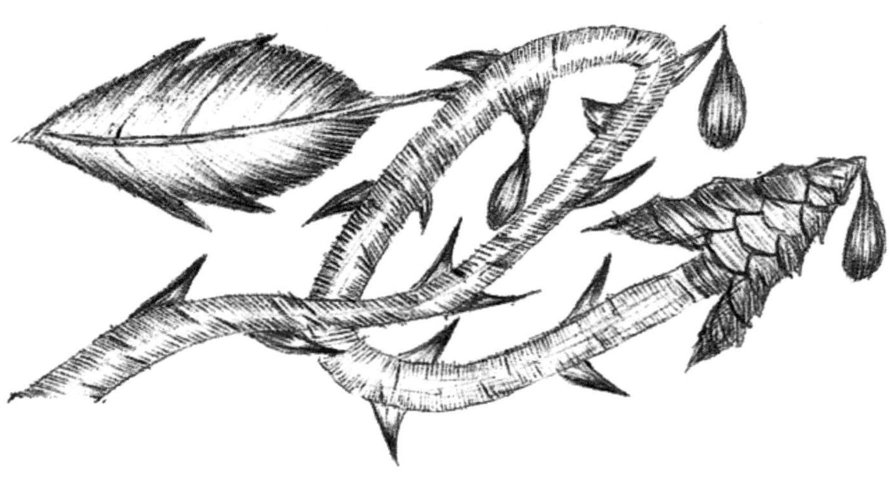

Martin wasn't evil. He would never rape, steal or hurt for the sake of it. Surprisingly, he was rather sensitive, kind, and oddly respectful given his "dangerous criminal" status. He'd done his share of bad shit, invariably under the influence, but to my knowledge Martin never killed anybody. I would venture to say he was capable, but only if circumstances backed him into a corner and there was no other way out. That sounds like self-defense but when you're a repeat offender of whatever, all is magnified, distorted and used against you. He would confide in me at random junctures. He ran away from his adopted parents; his father was a military man from the south. Now how did such a person end up adopting a little Indian boy from the Yakama Nation all the way out west? I never got a satisfactory answer to that but I didn't really think much about it until years later, trying to understand "my frind."

Martin's troubled life would seem almost destined from the beginning. Making his way back west with virtually nothing, he befriended another runaway and they robbed a gas station for a few bucks; I don't even think they were armed nor was it a felony but it was his first run-in with the law.

Another more serious offense took place while doing time. He got wind that a young cousin had been raped in another joint. How many times had I heard "what goes around comes around," by finger pointing hippies embracing karma? This was the real thing. He didn't kill the man but came close, at least that's what he led me to believe. Now he *was* a felon.

Years later on his way to Alaska to find a fishing job, that thus far had eluded him in midlife, he wanted to get laid before shipping out to sea. He arranged for a hooker that night; she shows up but "she" is a transvestite. Martin is not amused and says so—wants his money back. Not so easy, he starts to hassle with him; Martin puts a knife to his throat and says, "I don't want any trouble, just my money back so don't fuck around." Well, who knows what happened "the bitch" got cut in the neck but luckily survived... or so the story goes.

This time, he'd been arrested for assaulting a woman near Pike Place Market. Therein is a small park and a favorite hangout for Indians with a couple of large totem poles to boot. They were meant to celebrate the local Native Culture but in fact their origins are from other tribes, mostly north on Vancouver Island. Like the misplaced totems, Martin could never find a comfortable place to be—his Don Juan spot so to speak. The path of least resistance placed him in Seattle, quite a way from the territories of The Yakama Nation. As much as he had a very high regard for Native traditions, he was completely divorced from his own tribe even as an adult after making his way back to the west. He despised the res.

Given the police report it was easy to imagine what might have gone down. With a New Year's Eve hangover, Martin sees a young woman sitting on the park bench and asks for spare change. She says something insulting and Martin overreacts, grabs one of her earrings and yanks it clean from the pierced hole. He denies it; there are witness reports of someone in a white parka-like jacket; he doesn't have one. Otherwise it's a "he said she said" but when you're a Native with a record, you're fucked—plain and simple.

I went down to the market and asked around. Talked to a few Indian brothers, to no avail. All I got was a slurred, "you do the crime; you do the time." They gave him eight years, mostly due to his rap sheet, however, he did avoid the dreaded 3rd strike. This would turn out to be his longest prison stint by far. Paying for the attorney was the first real chunk of change I spent on Martin's behalf. Over time this guilty white man's token gesture turned into some serious money as I repeatedly bailed him out of drug-induced debt. He would invariably bury himself in too deep and owe nasty gangs that threatened pain and death if not paid. I justified the slew of CODs (code word: "tapes") by the fact I had sold an edition of *Facing Faces* and just maybe he deserved some of the profit.

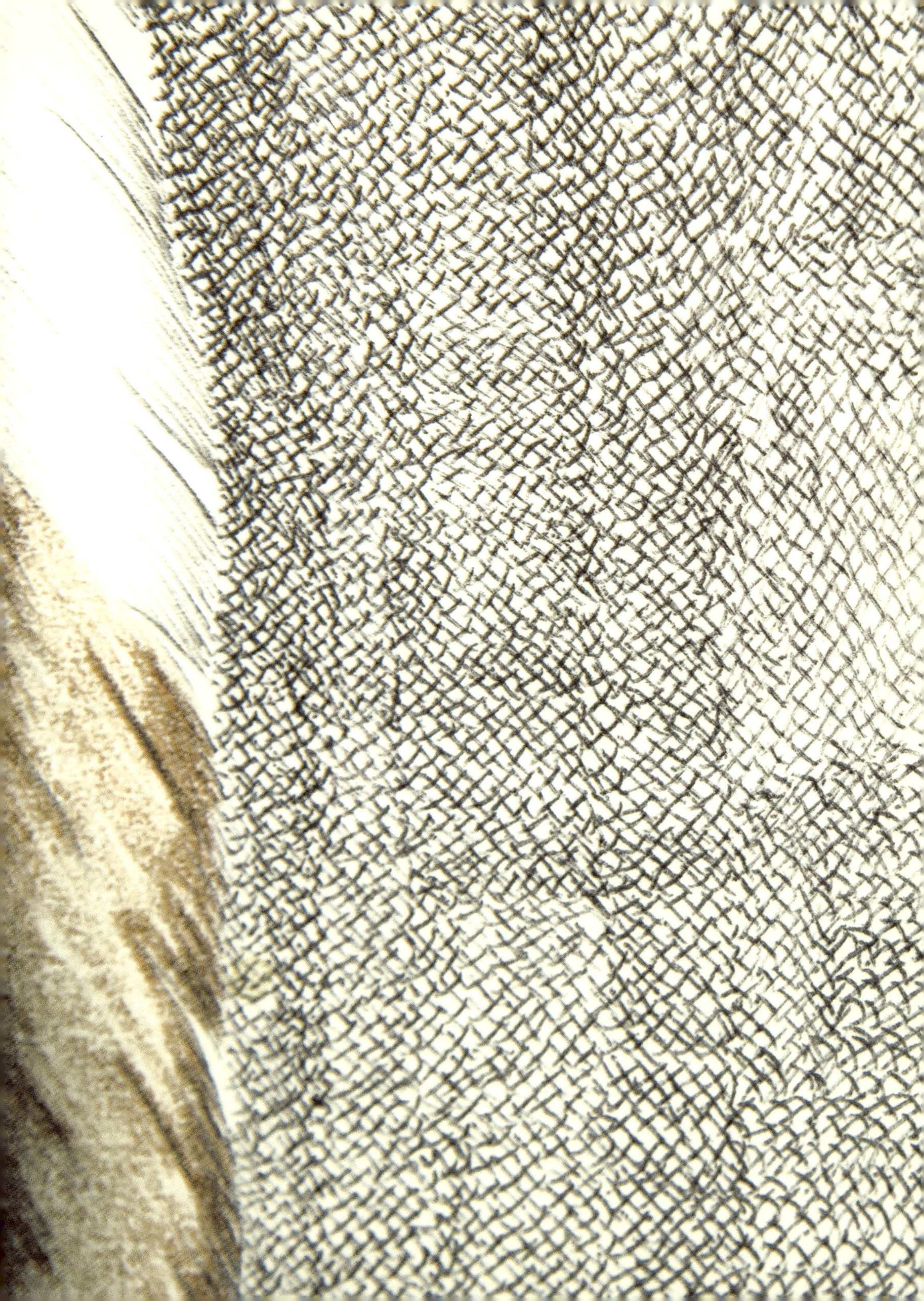

Hey How you doing. So your off to Europe huh!!
Well all i can say is be careful. My last snappy letter
i wrote you I wanted to get the picture out of here
my Generic work huh! huh! Sure was good to talk
to you   this place is a New prison   it's relly strange
here. I was not trying to call or write you on the
Holidays   I figure you needed to enjoy your Holiday
without some con writting in calling you all the time.
I feel like i'am harresing you, or your frind's think
i'am, just parinoid closeing in on   the wall's ha! ha!
Nothing to it   Man   It just makes me stronger at
heart   it's teaching me something but i don't kno
what, anger, depressed, parinoid, crazy, as a nut
ha! ha! This is what i think   don't crack be kool, be
strong, don't worry tell i get ware i'am going, tell i
get there i can make it out of here   I relly don't kno
what i'am going to do when i get out of prison   get
lay, and have something good to eat first day when i
get there. Pay off this Loan, then start putting money
up for a place   when i get out don't evan have
clothes crazy huh! i'am so in dept. Must get this tape
done. I don't kno what their going to do with me
Tire of time tho   How do you all like your Red Cross
now Ha! Ha! Rip off all those people   People should
of just pick out a family and gave it to them or help
or money persona f_ _ _ Red Cross   All dress up
wearing fancy clothes + jewlery make me sick, can
you beleave that crap. Last time they told me i was
getting out, they let me out, then took me to walla
walla in lock me up again   Now they bring me here
in now they say they might let me out again. You
could call your frind + check if he can fine out if their
going to let me out of the hoe or what + where is my
tv + clothes   i pay for it to be ship here in they never
let me kno if it's here or not   I relly would just like
to quit going from hoe to hoe you   you know what
i mean. I don't kno Gary   Forget it   i don't kno what

i want ha! ha! I here they have a proublem here
with people stuff comeing up missing plus book
+ magazine   my Neighbor get mags but they tell
him they don't kno where their at   Mail relly goofey
here. This hoe make's your body + mind waird i
think. Well hope you had a nice Thanksgiving + Nice
Christmas comeing up   I'm drawing a EAgle   It's
11:00 PM   I decided i should finish this letter today,
or tonight is the **4**th Dec   Jack so what have you
been doing Jack ha! ha! I'am watching Jack + the
Bean stock and drawing. I would never turn nobody
in for my freedom, He is the one in his world. I
would never betray you my frind   you are the only
one that has help me out since i've been lockup.
Ben is a warrior in his own world. I see it's snowing
on tv   has it snow in Seattle yet. I just got some new
sheet's + Blanket   they pass them threw the shoot
in the door, Exciteing in here. I don't kno what else
to write Gary   i'll let you get to your life   Take care
of the tape   how many minute are on it   why me!!??
Ha! Ha! Saw or heard the expression on tv   O.J. the
dope dealer   what a clown he is   he got everything
in he want's to come to prison   F_ _ _ ing Geek, Got
a big break in keeps pushing it. Well i'll close for
now, I reread my letter   I mean i'll get lay when i get
out of prison Ha! Ha!

Gary

Hello! So what's up's?? Not much is going on here   it's just boaring. It's change of season Equinox   I get to sweat **2** times this week   Nothing going on in the Josha tape's what happening? Are you alright. My check's are not here again   My fund have been deleated for **2** weeks. I no the state don't give us what we need. The money you send me will go on shoe's here. we can not order or get shoe's from the street's. I could use the coat if it does not have pocket's or one on the inside if it doe's you could take or have someone take out the pocket n no black lineing. I could use a couple pair of short's **3**xlarge and some socks and boxer and a couple beanie hat's wool and wool glove's nothing black and a couple wool xxlarge sweater tan or white Army surplus has cheap clothes. I thought about ordering here but other people say it cheaper if your people order them. So can you please help me with clothe's so when you leaving to Europe. Are you doing ok i hope your not depressed hope your women id fine. I was walking the yard at night n my cellie went to call his family when he was done he had tears on the corner of his eye's telling me all his nieces + nephews are starting to talk he talk to one on the phone you no children talk first words. He said to me i'am missing so much. Life is so hard for his young mind. I pray to my spirits to help him n i walk as i pray for you n your family i wonder when i die where do i go besides to the soil do you feel me. I think about that since i"am getting with age. My cellie's sleep all day stay uo for **7-8** hy and go back to sleep waird people. i got to get out, i feel like i'am losing it in this place. I hope you can take care of the C.O + send me some money for shoe's. This place is stressing. i will close for now your prison bum frind Ha! Ha!

      hope everything fine
      Your frind Martin

Send pictures
P.S. Did you get my Hand drum you can put it on your wall in your shop Natives made it hold on to it for me i'am working on your picture

Over the years Martin became aware of my susceptibility to depression. One never knows how, or why, and certainly not when the next bout will be. The dread rears from nowhere, as if it had a separate consciousness—one that stalks until complete surrender takes place. The talk of friends, lovers, acquaintances might touch upon brain chemistry imbalance, a devastating loss from the past, or hint at an onslaught of unfortunate extenuating circumstances. But unless they've "been there, done that," it's in one ear and out the other. The raison d'être to the depressed? —it don't matter.

Feeling a bit like I had set myself up for a fall that in all likelihood would transform into a full-blown breakdown, I went to the coast to take inventory of my precarious state in hopes of at least forestalling if not completely sidestepping a lurking madness that had already begun to dig its claws in. I took a cabin on the Quileute res, a relatively remote location in the Pacific Northwest. The tribe, known for its fishing, typically trolled deeper waters offshore—far enough to be out of sight beyond the horizon and then some, at least from the vantage point of my big picture window. As they return in the pre-dawn hours, somewhere among the starlight, Rayleigh scatterings and one's own acumen for patience, each vessel's light would "pop" over the horizon into view. One, two, then five more, another and so on; it becomes a fleet. For the tribe this is all in a day's catch. For me, it was the quintessential moment, uncannily double-sided, in which I saw myself either resigning to the throes of depression or my entire constitution being flushed and cleared in an epiphany of childlike wonder.

Artist unknown, Native American hand drum
(front with painted skin), circa 2000

Like others, alien to its crippling power, it was difficult for Martin to wrap his head around the dregs of depression. Granted, having not had the "opportunity" of a stay in the pen there was no way for me to gauge any kind of comparison. Perhaps he saw it as something like the white man's existential burden. Once the disease claims you, when you can't even lift yourself off the floor, this kind of hopeless despair becomes a prison all its own—the walls close in, every thought is met with innumerable counter thoughts; all is dry, opaque, colorless and numb.

In 2000-01, I was a fellow at the American Academy in Rome, preparing for a retrospective along with a catalog raisonné. I could say, you might say, "things are going well." And then there are those "extenuating circumstances." The place is stuffed with scholars walking around with their noses high in the air. My 15-year-old daughter decided to join me during the peak of her teenage angst, mild when compared to the entire spectrum of what's possible, nevertheless her troubles occupied a permanent space in my hurricane brain. When coupled with a high-strung girlfriend that sang a cappella in the moment at any moment while she worked on an album and persona called Pinky Lizardbrain, I felt like some kind of old tree. I drifted into the cliché habit of pacing the studio.

The day I turned 50 (and I could swear that had nothing to do with it) I'm walking in circles—from the outside a kind of meditation; from the inside, I was quickly losing contact with all familiarity, anything to keep me anchored was disappearing. I would remember something--a lamp, a chair, camera, anything--my mind became a killer—some kind of inversion was taking place. The space was beginning to radically undulate in scale increasingly extreme--I found myself crashing into objects, the furniture and the walls growing more violent as I continued. I feared that if I stopped moving, hesitated for an instant—my heart, breath and words would fail me—my mouth would seize up and my being would enfold like collapsed origami. The circles became ellipses and soon I wasn't sure where I was, or even if I existed at all; words and things were separating at breakneck speed. I was slipping into a kind of catatonic state. My girlfriend called a nearby homeopathic doctor. After a few words were exchanged, it was evident he wasn't equipped to deal with my condition and recommended a Dr. Bourne on the other side of town. He was a deeply caring older British man, a classic Freudian psychiatrist. I had no choice but to go as I was on the edge and close to suicidal. After just a few weeks of traveling via public transportation twice a week to his office on the outskirts of Rome (a back room of his apartment) I was at least safe from the absolute bottom, if only temporarily. He put me on Paxil which in retrospect saved my life but is a bitch to ween oneself from.

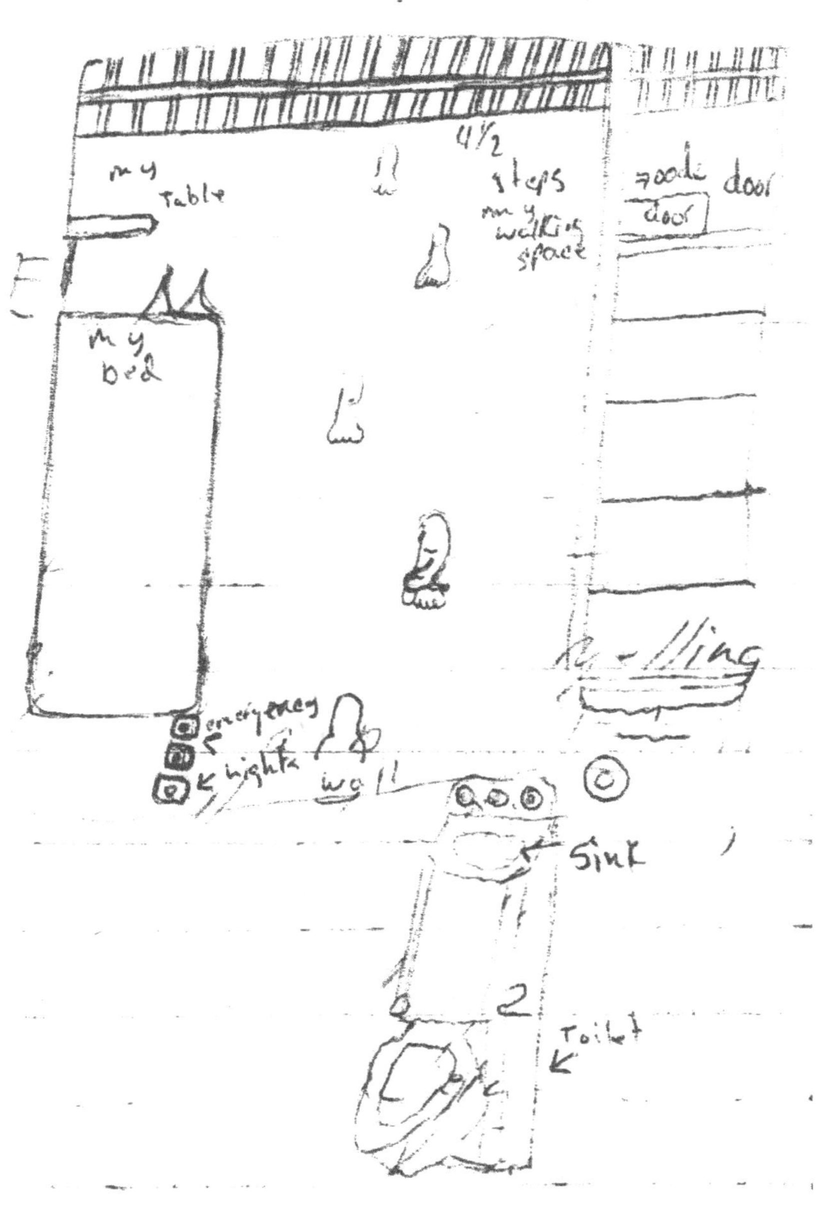

9798992
my cell
4 ½
steps
my walking space
food door
door
my Table
my bed
emergency
lights
wall
k-Wing
Sink
2
Toilet

55

Hello! What you doing? What you makeing a tv interview or show of you sound's interesting   Thanks for the picture of you and your woman   is this your California women   What kind of hairdo is that she has. She not bad looken. I guess anything you do date is as-in-female is better than anything i have   ha! Ha!   **5** finger Molly here ha! Ha! Like the ciggarette   wish i

could enjoy the luxery but to expensive here, cool glasses My mind is trying to stay strong, pure, mean, happy, sound strong!! This little cell is a killer   break you down if you don't watch it   I sing to myself Native song's   Rock music   Soul   Stuff i rember and draw alot and sometime's talking to my art   weird   i stay up all night drawing reading exerciesing walking my cell   i sleep all day   try to save my food for night time   i get up now at **7** and the evening, I get a 1hour of yard aday **2** to **3** times a week   outside feel good   it like a dog kennel crazy, sometime's they try to talk to me and get in my head the guards. I don't even talk to

LORRAINE JAMES

TOPPENISH - Lorraine James, 46, of Wapato, went to the Creator at

Toppenish Providence Hospital on Aug. 30. Lorraine was born Sept. 16, 1954, in The Dalles, Ore., to Harvey and Mamie (Wahpat) James Sr.

She was a lifelong Yakima Valley resident. Lorraine attended and graduated from Wapato High School. She then attended Yakima Community College. Lorraine was a member of the Yakama Nation and 1910 Shaker Church of White Swan.

She is survived by one daughter Priscilla James of Yakima, her father Harvey James Sr.; three brothers Harvey James Jr., and Martin James all of Toppenish; and Marvin James of White Swan; three sisters Virginia James of Mont.; Priscilla James of Tacoma; and Amber James of Toppenish; numerous nieces, nephews and cousins. Lorraine was preceded in death by her mother Mamie Wahpat James and two sisters Mary and Darcy James.

Dressing services were held Aug. 31 in Merritt Funeral Home Chapel. Following the dressing services she was moved to the 1910 Shaker Church at White Swan for overnight services. Funeral services were held early morning Sept. 1, with concluding services and burial in the 1910 Shaker Church Cemetery near White Swan.

them, they ask me how i'am doing and i just look at them   they put my food and a shoot in the door like a dog arf! arf! (The top book must be tooken care of   it's called, massie elder, do you understand   no add i'am in the hoe can you feel me bro   don't lose add of   First can't keep thin's like the here

i hope you understand   I herd someone just say where's the
pill man. They give out sleeping pill's like mad down here
Keep these people pretty down + out, not trying to get there
my neighbor take them. The cop's and the Health worker
was giveing my next door neighbor his ding Biscuit and saw
me looking at them and said here your sleepin pill's. I think
to my self no thanks danger zone zombie time Ha! Ha! Fell
alseep once   thAt's why i'am here sleeping at the party ha!
ha! Chrystelle sent me some post card's   only thing i had to
look at down in the hoe   now i have your picture thank's   i
put them up when i go jogging in stair at them as i jogg in
place   sometime's i go jogging at **2** or **3** in the mouring. Every
other day i do tow touches   **300** so a set   **380** to **400** stomich
crunches plus strach + leg kick's front + back knife. Second day
workout **570** pushup more crunches pacctice tie-quan-doe
for a hour or so   that's my routine down here, like the picture
what kind o coffee is that   like what's sitting next to you ha!
ha! Sept **11**, herd what happen after i ate   they put a memo
on the floor by my door telling about thoes f_ _ _ _ _ _ _ a_ _h_
_ _ that sent terrorist here to hurt people   i feel bad for them
all, same day i recived a paper from my rez telling me my sister
die on Aug **31** and they bury her on the **1** of Sep   That one
was a good sister   she had lupis diease   I used to live with her
in alaska plus in puylip   she would send for me all the time to
come stay with her so i would go cruise her around alot   When
i first came to washington my sister had me stay with her   i was
a stranger to her   she knew me but i did not knew her. skip relly
wuick, when i lived over seas in the **60** i rember crossing the
field's and looking at the jungle grass up to my knees   i was
amaze with the beauty but also intimated by what i could not
see when i was walking or what was in the bush or jungle.

WASHINGTON STATE PENITENTIARY
SUPERINTENDENTS MEMO
September 11, 2001

TO: Inmate Population

FROM: John Lambert, Superintendent

RE: Terrorist Attacks

Several areas of the United States were attacked this morning by terrorists, responsible parties have not yet been identified.

They hijacked several commercial airplanes and crashed them into the two World Trade Center Towers in New York City and another into the Pentagon Building in Washington DC. A forth crashed somewhere in Pennsylvania killing all aboard without hitting a target.

These events will not effect the daily operations of Washington State Penitentiary. Information will be forthcoming if there is a change in our daily routine.

How it' going Mary

It's good to hear From you Yes the slaughter has begone. Always for all mankind to ki' each other sooner or later damn shame. I trying to draw + write you at the same time So what you working on your birthday is near So say Happy Birthday now cause you will proubly be gone quickly to your new Gig as you say I got lost in the Bead's their long tittious work. So i put it to the side for a little bit in draw For you your pictur i said i would. im apolizizeing So how's your women doing So she don't think war's great to battle other countries. Life is full of amazement's as you kno already It's been rainey up here + windy tittious in the Unit main line. It's breakfast here is another day upon us here tick tock the day passing the insinites Start's around + around

Yes the slaughter has begone   Always for all mankind to kill each other sooner or later damn shame. I trying to draw + write you at the same time... I got lost in the Bead's their long tittious work. So i put it to the side for a little bit n draw for you your pictur

How it' going Gary

It's good to hear from you   Yes the slaughter has begone. Alway's for all mankind to kill each other sooner or later damm shame. I trying to draw + write you at the same time. So what you working on   Your birthday is near   So i say Happy Birthday now cause you will proubly be gone quickly to your new Gig as you say   I got lost in the Bead's   their long tittious work. So i put it to the side for a little bit in draw for you your pictur   i said i would, i'am apolizigeing   So how's your women doing   So she don't think war's great to battle other countries. Life is full of amazement's as you know already   It's been rainey here + windy   Attion in the unit main line. It's breakfast here is another day upon us here   tick tock   the day begins   the insinitey start's   around + around   The yard is closed again **4** day's now   looking for Knife's or shank's they call it here. I had three pieces of pancake in grapefruit   Breakfast at the Ritz ha! ha! . Monday mourning   Sometimes I feel out of touch with everything. I explain me in alot of my family don't get along because of my father offering me land before my other family member's   they did not loook at that with open eye's or hearts. So i left   Never went back   only to see my children   I left for the city to find my Gold. Only thing i found was a loss of dignity + my pride

Alcohol drug's we that at the Rez too   But no money. I explain also my family could give a f_ _ _ if i live or die   That is why i don't hang around them   Our blood isn't that fool of love   when i left i left   now i'am on my own   Native are not like people think we should be   we survived off our pass in we will never forget what people did to us in our land   made to walk for miles + ride in cattle car's with no food + water   my ancestor dying in being left   i stand away from my people on my own trying to survived in make it   it would take a life time to explain my or life. If i say to much people would not understand me It hard to learn New thing when you think you No it all. You don't **1/2** to come visit me Gary   this is not a good place Gary   exspecialy after our last visit   I could of never mind   I was so happy to talk to you i forgot to ask did you get that paper work i sEnt you of why they took my Good time. I don't kno mister this is a crazy place   my thought's are my throught's   I'am waiting for my freedom. Later mister
Where you off to next   Later   Martin Cothren

My relationship with Martin fluctuated radically between wanting
to help him in every way I could and completely cutting ties
which, over time I realized wasn't going to be possible. There was
something *I* needed from *him*. Hard to say what that was other than
maintaining contact with a life that was completely Other than
mine. Indeed, from the outside he was exotic, a Native American
convict with a deep spiritual vein—something I felt I've always
lacked in certain ways.

It was easy to imagine our obsessions tracking one another.
Every couple of months I would receive a drawing from Martin,
typically with Native iconography embedded with secret symbols
and rituals. Some being so intricate they produced a considerable
amount of pareidolia. At the time I was traveling extensively,
doing exhibitions and talks mostly in Europe and some elsewhere.
Somehow, I managed to take calls or return his calls, all of which we
assumed were being monitored. We established a few code words for
things that could get him written up. I could speak backwards fairly
adeptly, something I learned from a work I'd done, *Why Do Things
Get in a Muddle?* I tried to teach Martin "forget the letters, think
sound" to no avail. We managed and what we couldn't communicate
we dealt with during following visits.

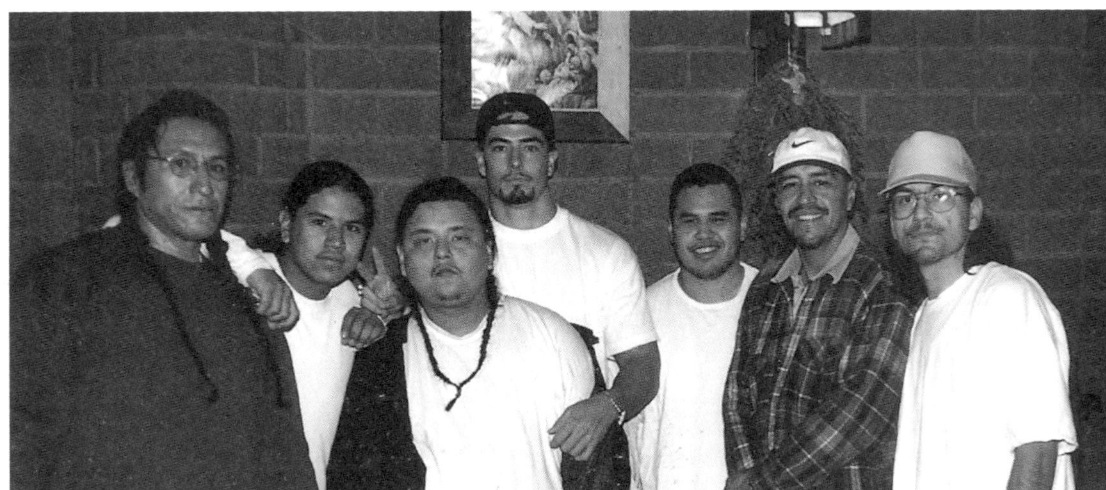

Martin Cothren (furthest left) with cellie and Native associates

Being a little over an hour from Seattle, the Monroe Correctional Facility was the only place I was able to visit Martin. After a few years they had moved him so many times I lost track; Colorado, Arizona, several locations in Washington State with Walla Walla being the last stop.

When doing a prison visit, you are thoroughly processed like cattle: Everything out of your pockets, stand and wait in line until instructed to march through a metal detector; cold stares from guards standing around every step of the way; then through a second metal detector, followed by getting a stamp on your wrist; through a door into a hermetically sealed chamber, the door closes and another door opens—similar to some banks. The wrist is checked under a UV light and you've finally arrived. At this point, whatever dignity you thought you had is long gone; you've become a prisoner yourself and may now enter the visiting zone. Surprise visits caught Martin off guard; he was visibly moved that someone cared enough to take the time and go through the prison visit rigmarole in order to see him. One Christmas I arranged for a visit. He arrived at the visiting room wearing a long sleeve white shirt, his customary braids groomed to a tee. He acted like I would if going to visit grandparents during holidays. It wasn't just him being on good behavior, he wanted to make an impression—show that he was thankful. All told, we must have consumed over a hundred candy bars from the most expensive vending machine on the planet. And that's after they take 30% from every penny one receives from the outside, at least in Martin's case.

CELL WARNING		
Cothren Cell #	2-26-L	
Date:	6.30.02	
Make bed		
Clean Bars		
Sink & Toilet		
Unauthorized Box		
Unauthorized Items On Wall	Pictures cover More than cork board	
Privacy Curtain		
Excess Property		
Clean/Sweep floor		
Clean Desk Area		
Empty Trash		
Unauthorized Items In Cell		
Other		

FAILURE TO OBSERVE THESE RULES WILL RESULT IN AN INFRACTION

J Cook   Shift I

officer

Hello Gary

How it going   i hope fine. Thank you for the denairo   Not much going on
here   just trying to be stress free ha! ha! State keep's trying to break me
down make me crack   went to a Eagle ceremony at the sweatlodge   It was
very mind opening + very touching   the thought's that ran threw my mind
where the Eagle been in it's life before he met the big chill freezer. I stood
in listen to the Red people that day, say i thank you Brother for perticipating
with us   They talk of religion   then they talk about they are going to die
here   never to get out of prison again   I saw a few tear's that day in our
heart's + prayer. I just went to breakfast   i sit in front of this door   they say
i can't where my sweatshirt down there anymore   it get's cold down there.
I'am a little frustrated   i see the guard's down there in coat's all warm. So I
will where my coat tell they go no more coat's to the chow hall. Their closing
down this place very tight with their rules. **2-17-02** Thave tooken our lodge.
hour's from us today   they wanted to take away our bread + peanut' butter
+ jelly for our food when we come off of our **3** to **4** day fast sweatlodge Sun
rise Survices. I'am staying low i work in the lodge area. I just came back from
the lodge   this guy stood outside all day with us at the lodge watching us
more like peter gazeing watching naked people, watching us sweat   i sent
some stuff there for you   **2** madallion   **2** key turttle   **1** set babby moccison
i made a couple Earring set >< plus **1** ivory Earring set   put aside with the
clay pottery for me   other stuff is yours   Merry Christmas   They won't send it
to you for a week or two   Happy Belated Christmas present   all i could give,
rest i look at arn't to good.

I hope you quit bullshitting and come visit me one day like you keep saying
i'll be waiting

Later Mar
Merry Christmas
Happy New Year

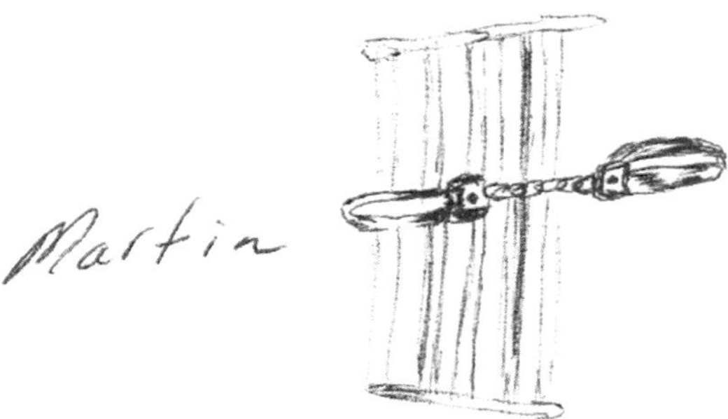

Martin

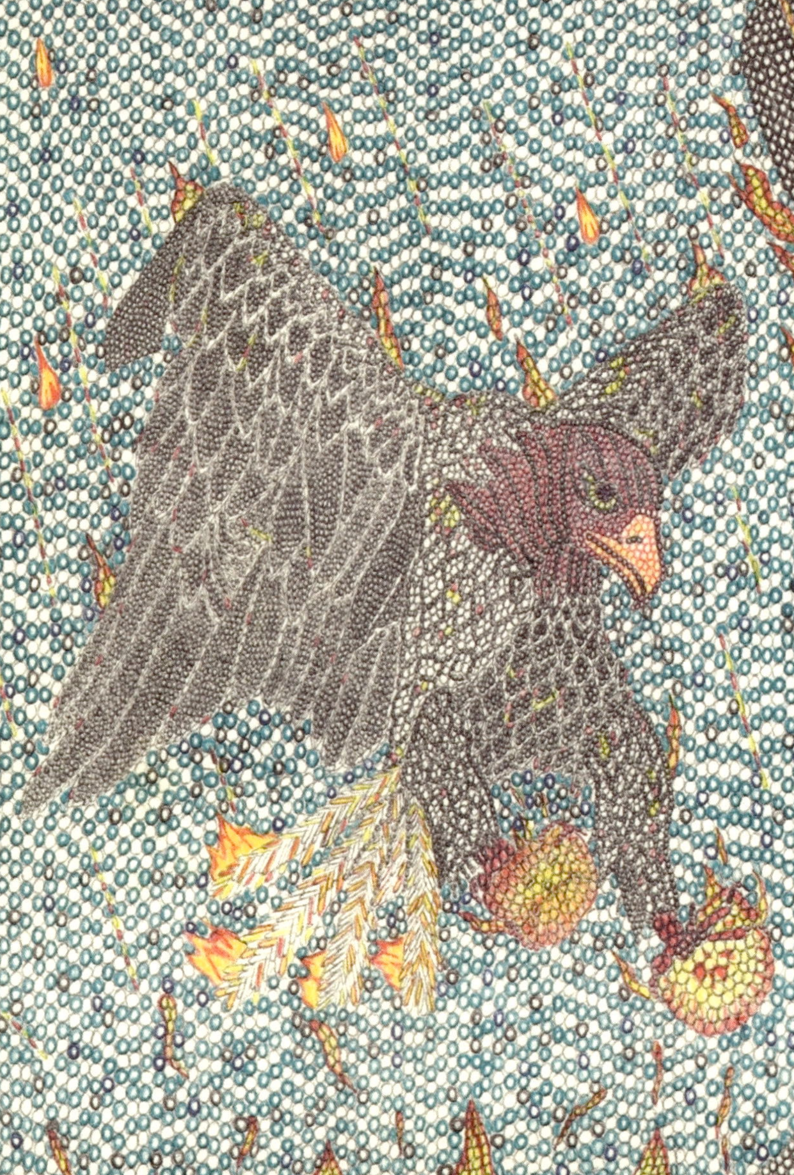

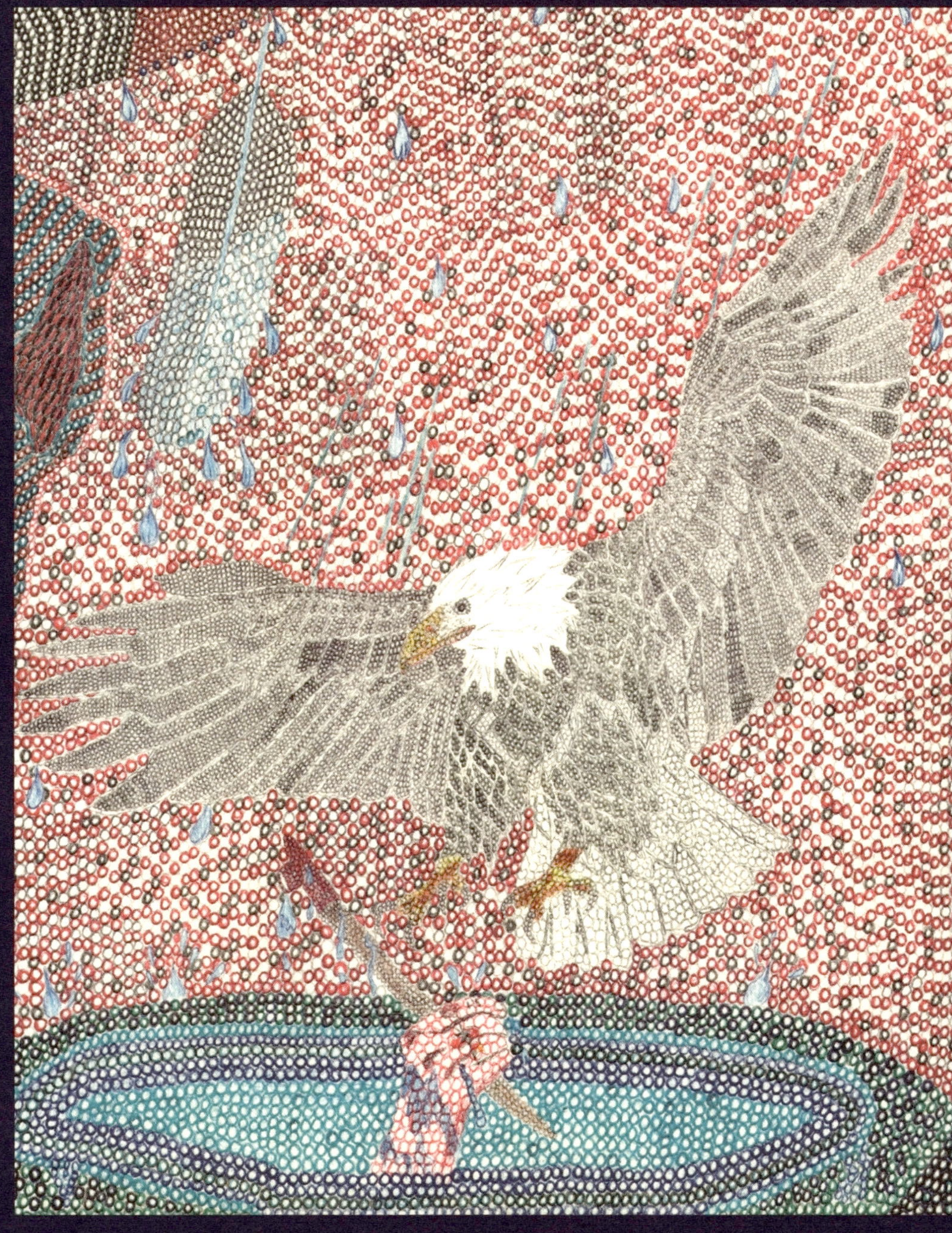

Woke me up at the last count said i was going to Ad Seg on wed **4:30** pm. friday at **8:30** on was on a bus to Walla Walla. They pick up **16** Indian's in just move us gave us a bullshit bogus write up. They pickup people that don't evan hang around the Indian's much. The write up said we were a threat to the religion changes they are having there that we were grouping up

They are fool of s_ _ _ , So i spent my birthday in the hole I feel like shit Their Lieing hard. My pen on a blink keep spotting My pen's no good. I am just laying here Listing to these people storie's all day Have not had a shower in **4** day's had to sneak a phone call **5**'am trying to hang in there Woke up early people hollering in vent. It's breakfast + Sunday mourning. What you doing i think of you sitting drinking coffee on a outside cafey something like that Looks like a shorties <- writting mean's child writting I'am trying to fix this useless pen it is acting up i evan try the soap in the pen back where it open at no Luck. I'am back in the penta where they shoot people in kill them "Oh Shit." I seem to be going backwords instead of forwards They pick me up for being native and for my record. I don't No I'am just spectating It's a night mare. Oh Hell when you think your about there Another wild card comes up. I'am a loser baby, so why don't you shoot me Ever herd that. It's going to cost more money to have my stuff sent to me. I walk i sit i think what to write

couple more month's i was going to put in for my Good time back   Here i sit in this negative wave path Nothing positive in it. I like the scenery over the pass in the snow. My two Neighbor just came in on Thursday their trying to get out of here Their scard of the Yard This is the place that kill some people in the last year crazy i found a pen Gary i had to stay up tell late at night to get this pen I'am writting you + ~~Chr~~ Christal or Chrystal or Cristal at the same time Christal which one April **4** finely. Send address Chrystal or ask her to write me Thank you   So how's Jimmy been doing? Tell him i said High   I'am just sitting here waiting fo a letter from you Where i can buy some envelopes and shampoh cosmetics. They said on the chain bus here **48** hr n we will be out we've been in here forever for doing nothing just being Indian's. Thank's for excepting my phone call's. So when are you leaving again   I'll call your secetairy if they move me again if your not around or emergency ok or write ok Gary   No TV or Radio here. Find anything on your porn surf interesting ha! Ha! your i don't know what to say Ha! Ha! Just waiting for you to send me a letter + picture i'am boar   I would proubly go crazy if i could not draw it occupy my mind. I'am trying to keep my mind strong. Keep on a strong mind. I can't beleave this crap I'am doing leg raise right now looking how fat i am getting so i begin my **1/2** ass workout in my little cell

The magazine is called <Native People> i don't no where you can buy it but i kno they have a web site. I rember certain thing my family don't rember then they kno thing's i don't kno here a piece of paper put it up in my litte cedar box can you lamatnate it first it's who i'am gary part of my family in the passing the life that went by as i sat mobil in one aera area enough about my sister but look hard at the paper i hope you catch the drift in the word in name my life is a Riddle sometimes. My heart is Heavy right now about her today is the **12** i did not feel nothing at first now i write you about her i start to feel my loss most quit writing for while I relly sorry i can''t be there for what ever i've only been to **2** funeral in my life but i'll see her when i get there you kno what i mean, Well they just turn off the light in the holl way or tier block it's around **10** pm   Christmas is nearly here again another year parish befor our Eyes for me like heat wave's in the desert i hope to be out of here one of these years ha! ha! What do your frind's think when i called and they here penitentiary Ask you what the hell your doing hanging around somebody like ~~me~~ him do they get the creeps or willie's ha! ha! I appricate you writting me Gary you make my week for a while Something to read something to look at, I'am drawing the picture again i like it so i'll proubly draw it over and over Think i could some money off of these little picture   i think there money in them exspecialay since it's ink freehand can you staiten them out n hang them. Who Are they Gary the sculpture is it Jesus + Mary is it Religion   I like them it's a challenge   You Need to hire your self a private plane to travel, in the way you travel arownd, more safer plus get yourselfs some weapon's nice Rifle or pistol you will need them in the feature out there. other country's are getting braver about testing out America. Crazy out there let me out. I just got done working out did my pushup crunches and toe touches ate half sandwich + **2** piecs of cakes good hole here ha! ha! I still trying to grasp what happen with my sister, and thoes planes Humen bein cease to never amaze me It's like me i seem to never quite amazeing my self I am talking life in general. It's relly not hard to beleave it happen i guess look at what people did to the Jews and the Native + Blacks My mom use to tell me never put all your money in one bucket or pocket There goe's those Tower's now they'll proubluy ~~arent~~ want to raise bill's every where store prices   I was thinking they proubly lost as many there as they did over sea and Nam in a hour   wild huh   i hope all your frind's + people are well, was not there in that. I stay up all night and stay asleep all day woke up n they were handing me your letter or Cartta about **7** or **8** at night   I've been in the Rubic Cube for a month

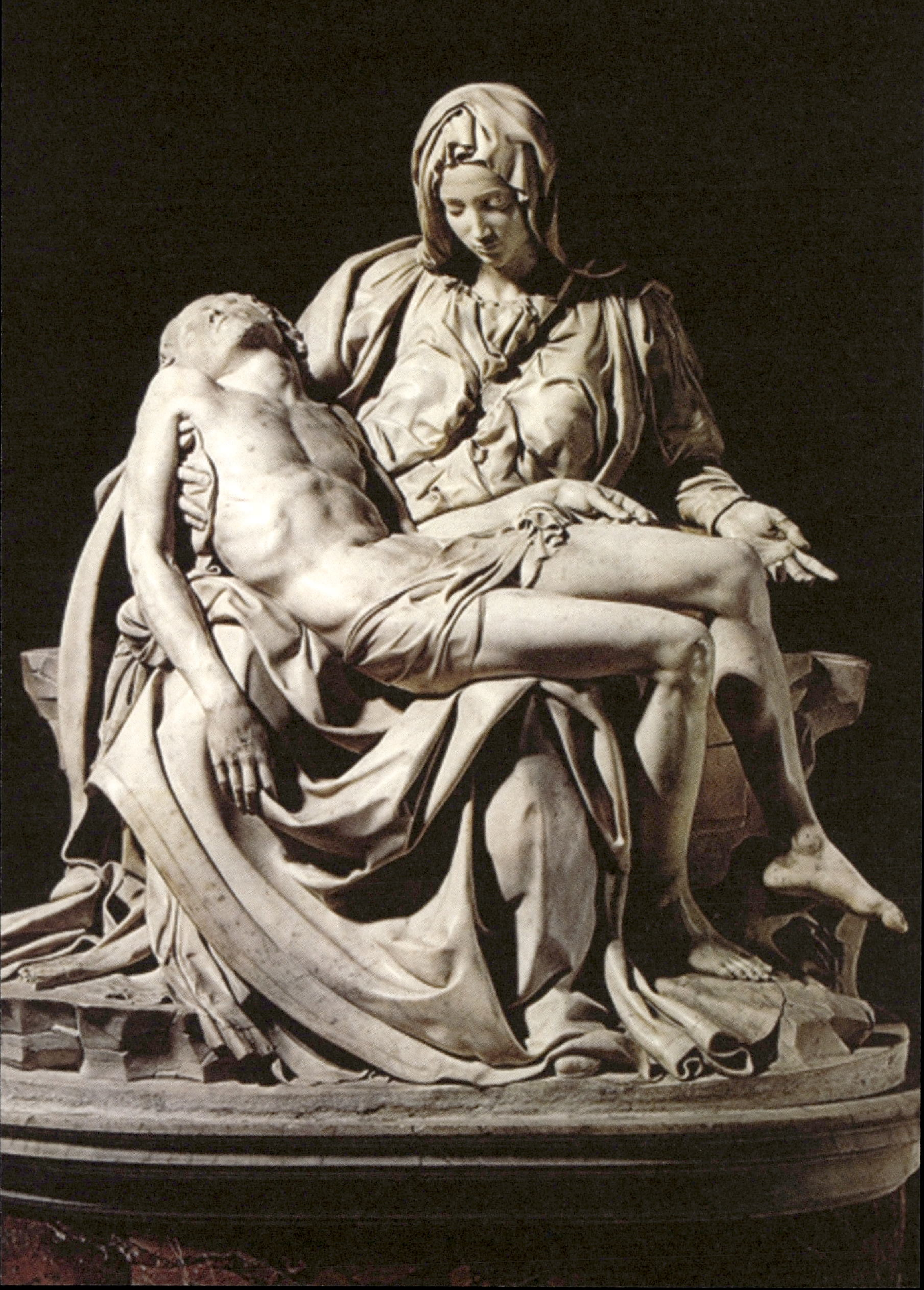

1/2 It's **2** mourning time to work on my picture It's **6:30 5** hr i work on the picture. Today is shower **10** min n outside yard fresh Air yea!! Just like a child but diffrent i have nothing, n they make me appricate a shower + yard creepy huh! Still be asleep about **9:00**AM wake after lunch go to my yard, OH yea Thank's for the money n picture Rember first one never replace add hope you got it still

So how is your women treating you huh! huh! How old this one   is she the one that make's your toe's curl up Ha! Ha! I'am going to keep Drawing this untel i can turn it into a Native Design   There so ~~many~~ much Dept in this i can't touch   i'am going to try tho   I feel i can do something with this picture i will try over + over   crazy huh! Hey is that a wig she wearing, Plus your hair's gettin long. Gary you've been a frind since i've been doing time in fact the only one takeing care of me so don't ever think the oppsent   however you spell <-. The hoe is just trying to work me down   I'am not trying to be in your way you kno what i mean, what you smokein there   one of those French cigg Well i'll call it a day   read some of this book   go to sleep untel shower + yard loseing weight in these f_ _ _ _ _ _ hole's. When i did that **18** days at airway in the hole i drop from **248** + **225**   that quick they starve you here   Maybe they have that magazine in the book store at i forget the name   I'am out of here   write you befor i send this out. Sept.**13** Went to yard this evening feel's nice out   **7:45** already dark out   won't see yard for a couple of days now or shower   oh well   life's a bitch   Called Thursday to see if your ok   not much i could do - if you was in New York- anyway hope your well   Enjoy your surfing   I shell close this for now,   Let you get back to your world   Enjoy the Fall weather   Expand your mind   Hope you find the Magazine Native People What kind of music are you to Gary   Raggay or Rock   what do you listen to in paris or Italy. Take care! Gary! be safe out there   you + your family have a Good Life out there to the fullest   peace out my friend

   got your picture's on my wall

   keep me with realtey sometimes
   wall's close in on me

Michelangelo, *Pietà*, 1498-1499
St. Peter's Basilica, Vatican City

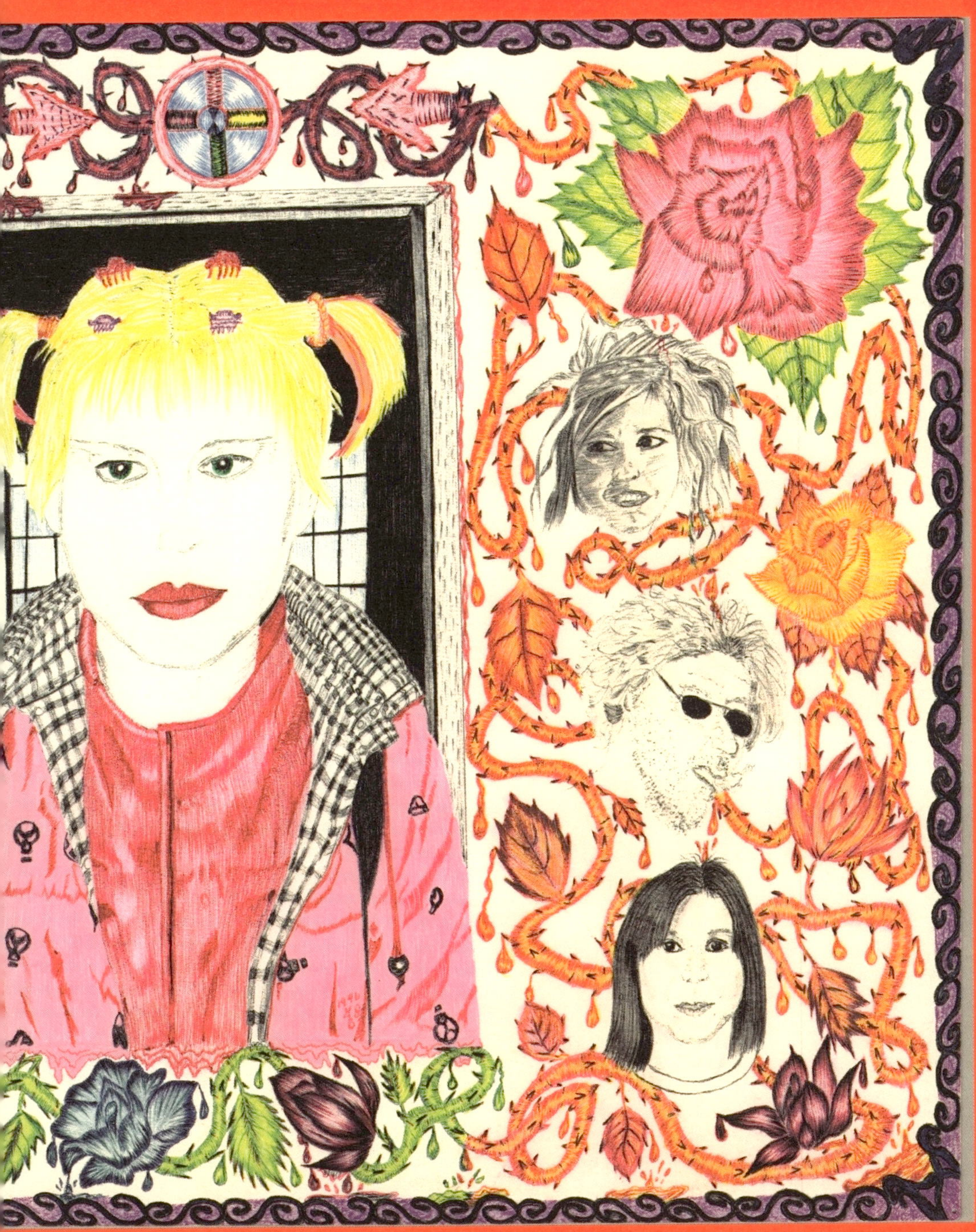

"Have you seen Jimmy lately?" I don't know how we came
up with the "code" name—nothing special about it. Over a
couple of years of visits and sharing stories--aside from our
peripheral connection through art, we shared the usual drug
talk, especially of the psychedelic variety. When it came to the
vices, he wasn't selective one iota and would take anything to
escape the prison mindset. Even on the outside—the same. For
Martin, he was always imprisoned except perhaps when he was
drawing and later beading. I had done my share of drugs, both
hard and soft, but acid has always been a kind of saving grace;
something to take inventory with now and then. At one of
many junctures along the way, I was desperate with no money
to speak of. Through questionable Woodstock acquaintances,
I got involved in growing pot and eventually storing about
40 duffle bags of hash in my closet for a few months (I had
to dump a couple of cans of fresh coffee grounds on them to
camouflage the smell). It was apparent this made me more legit
to Martin—that I had done something that could have landed
me in prison for a long time. This was especially true in that it
took place in New York during the "war on drugs." One night
watching the local news there was a report of a bust in the
neighboring town of Catskill. Undercover cops were carrying
out the *same* duffle bags I had. I panicked and thought to take
the whole load down to the Hudson river and dump it. Never
really knew whose it was—I could have been worse off than just
getting busted. I managed to contain the fear and eventually
somebody picked it up and handed me a brown paper bag with
twenty-grand in cash... Nice lunch if I do say so myself.

This built trust from Martin's point of view. So, when I came up with
a plan to smuggle him some acid there was no second guessing. "There
will be two stars on either side of your name, signaling it's in the letter."
In would mean blotter under the four corners of the stamp. I must
have done this at least five times and not without trepidation and a
little paranoia. Hard to imagine dosing in prison; hard to imagine
being in prison period. Martin was in the "hole" a lot, or so it seemed.
Every other letter I received he mentioned being in the "hole."

Gary!

Hope this letter finds you well. I proubly should have taken
your gold when I could have ha!ha!
Why dont you bring that music from Jimmy n we can share
some when you visit. During holidays they allow more time
maybe **3**. **4** hours

When I realized what Martin was saying I began to perspire and feel
queasy, not unlike coming on to a decent hit. Suddenly my thoughts
were ricocheting off the walls...they will know; they will see us fucked
up; the dose will be larger than expected; I'll freak out; Martin will
freak out; maybe he'll get violent, start throwing the chairs; cause a
prison riot; the guards will pull their guns; Martin and I will hit the
ground and start laughing uncontrollably; I'll get arrested right there
and they'll lock me up and throw away the key. Safe to say my mind
was reeling. The very next day I smuggled in two hits of blotter...

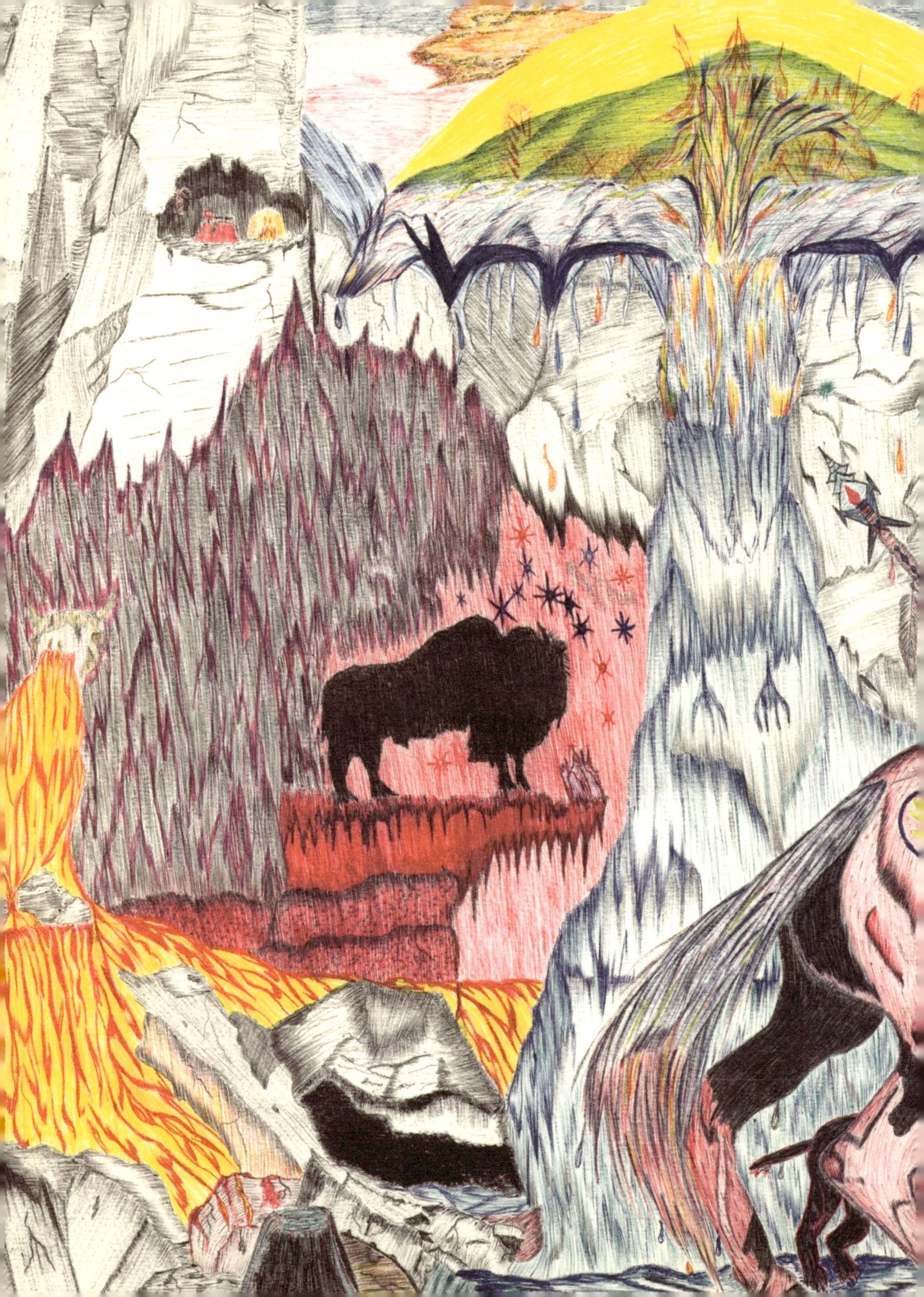

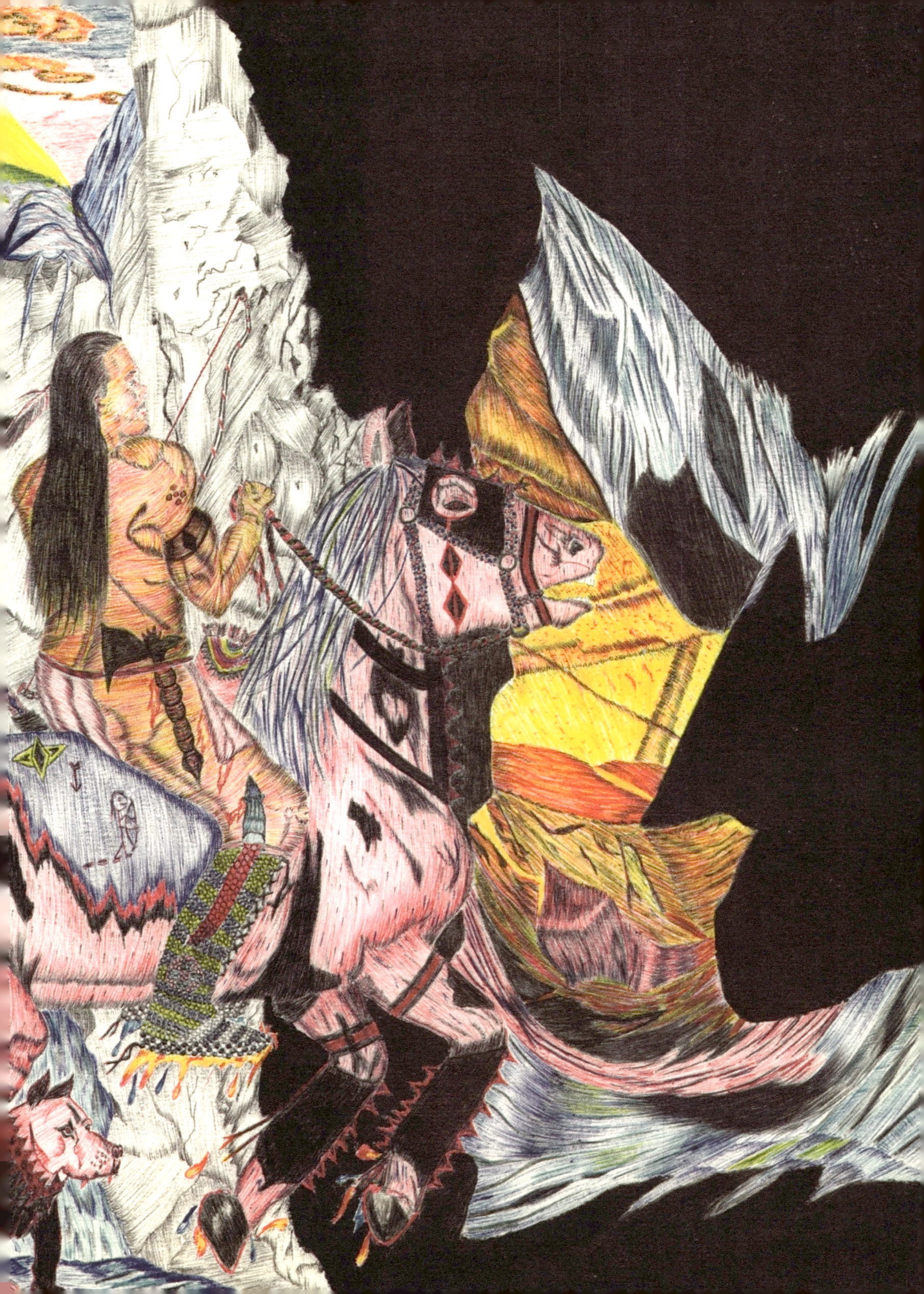

Hello Gary

More rule's Ha! Ha   hope Everything's fine   So you been surfing   Thank's for the letter + picture + denairo. Your picture of the surfer is on the wall   i look at it everyday studing it. wish i could do face's. I don't understand, can draw except the person face. It would be nice to have a visit from you. I'am still in the computer class   slow learning for me. It's hot in these cell's or just mine   didn't order a fan this year   This place is insane   a couple of cop's got the shit kick out of them. Now they kno how we feel   i got to live in this shit. I hung all your pictor on my board where i can look at them. So your getting ready for Europe   great   Be safe n Enjoy   There alot of two people in here   Gary burn a hole in your back. **I 5:30** in the mourning   listing to the silence. Now everybody wakeing up   I here all the toilet's flushing in all the sink going   people snoaring   listening to the gates being open   this is a old prison   all bars listeing to the Guard's   walking around listening to old new's on tv   murder, war's, + rape's, fire, the president, people starving, late night, Sat + Sun, people being save, Jerry Spring circus tv world. I watch these Guard's   They think their the toughest   their either getting beat up or beating up somebody or torching them physically or mentaly Ha! Ha! As-the inmate's world turns. Their the Indian are alway's trying to beat up their own people or take thing's from each other   i try not to talk much to them   their just problems or rumor to me. breakfast Mister   Later. Back we had **2** slice's of French Toast, **1** small bowel of oatmeal, This stupid guy try to fight me this weekend   Their gone here crazy so i watch what i say to people in prison here   He said he wanted to fight because i'am always interfering in people confersation + that i think i'am better them everybody Ha! Ha! I was going to fight him but said to myself Fuck him. he a person that look's for people that's weak or by their self   him n his frind's   he had to go around beating up people + old people he just got out of the hole for beating up a real old guy about **55** or **60**   oh well. I'am not worry he's some skinny bastard plus he's sick lukiema or something   I think he screw up in the brain's from prison. I'am gone to from prison but i'am not going around beating up people Ha! Ha! They save me a pair of glasse's in the hole without kno seeing a doctor and i can't evan see with these. So that's why i sent you my prescription   I argue in a kite to the Dr he said no. I went in sean my counsilor he got it approved you can send glasses in for me   he ask me a week ago   did i get them yet, i told him kno their tighten this place down so when you can i would appricate them befor they stop thing from the street's.   Take care Gary

1. <u>CELL INSPECTIONS</u>

- You are expected to be out of, and have your bed made by 7:30 a.m., unless you are on a medical lay-in or are a graveyard worker (if you worked the night prior), Monday through Friday of each week.

- Monday through Friday, you must have your cell cleaned and ready for inspection by 8:00 a.m. You will exit your cell when the officer enters to conduct a cell inspection. Unit officers will normally inspect the cells for cleanliness between 8:00 a.m. and 11:00 a.m. Cells are expected to be kept clean and in accordance with the unit rules at all times. Any failure may result in a general infraction.

- Saturday and Sunday, you must be out of bed and have your area cleaned and ready for inspection by 10:30 a.m. Normally, cells will be inspected between 10:30 a.m. and 1:30 p.m.

2. <u>BEDDING</u>

- Sheets are to be used on the mattress, and pillowcases on the pillow(s). Blankets will be covering the bed, pulled tight over the mattress, tucked in on both sides and at the head and foot. If a second blanket is issued, it will be folded at the foot of the bed.

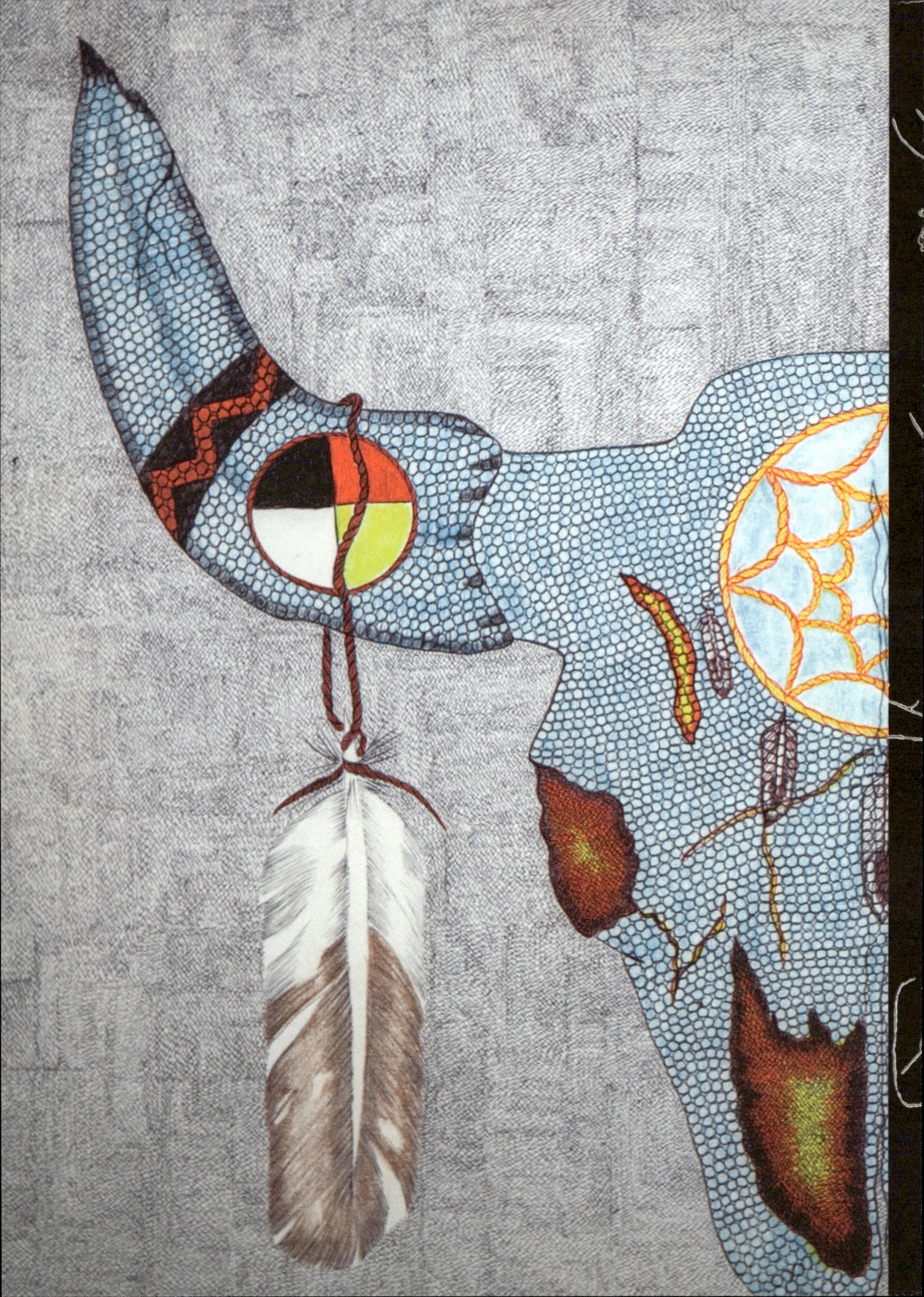

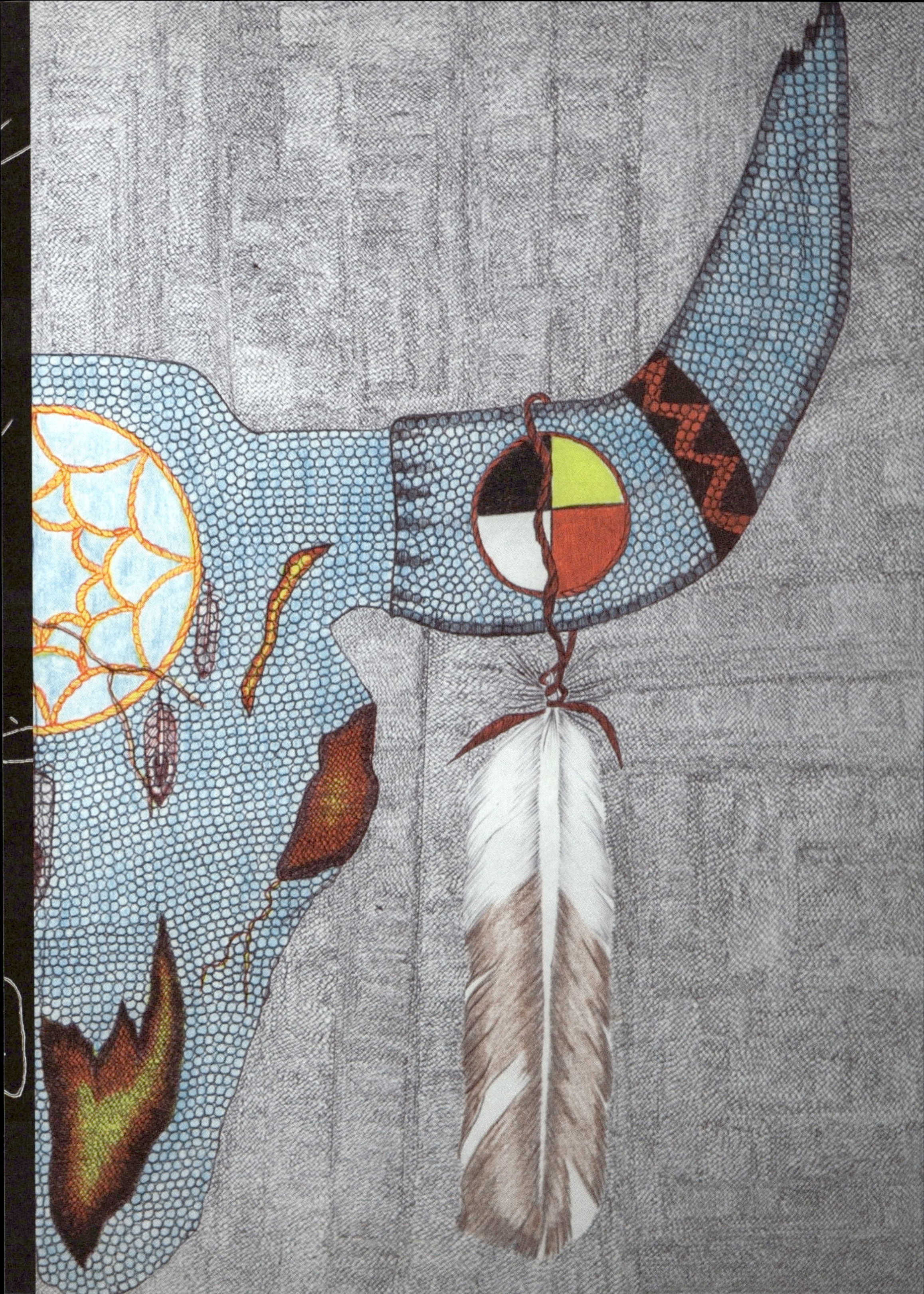

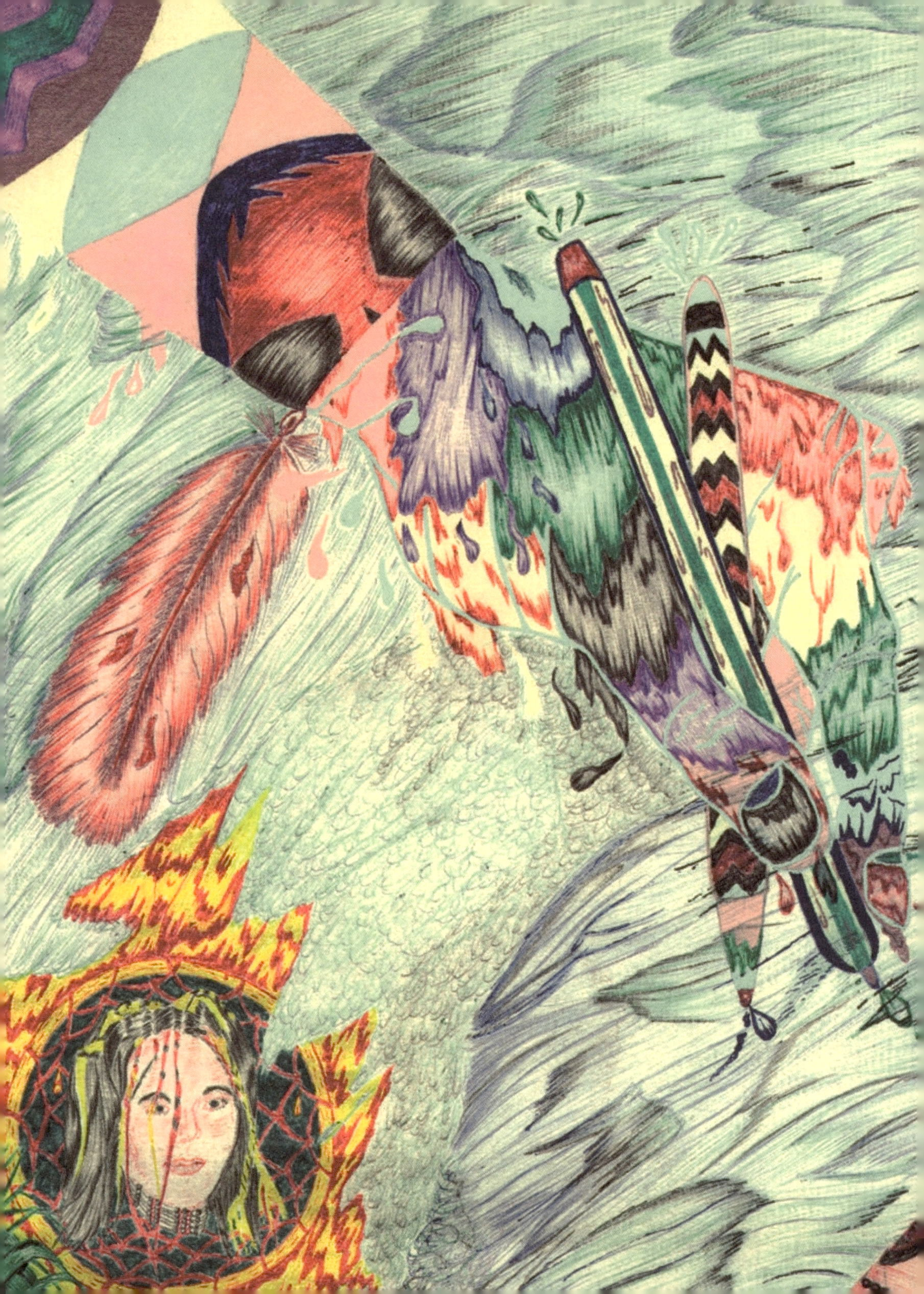

What ever happen, happen. then here's a couple
addresses for those book's if you can

If i live i don't know how i can ever relly repay you
if you relly kno what i mean. Sure would like to see
you But were so far apart   I am a Mess right now
and the mind still drug free the only thing good
about this. i,ve made a mess out of my pass life
Ha! Ha! The world i'll neve see but the TV from in
here   I thought every thing was ok but the past
has come up finely
When i came here to the wall's i got so paranoid
the **2** day i was in could not sleep from people
wanting thing i stay up all night with a massive
head ache and puke two times that night and said
to myself i can't run no where hang in there when
they come they come   This place is serious here
they have guards that sit in the tower with rifle
when you go to chow they have guards that sit in
there with rifles this is the death zone a week ago
a Native Kill himself in the hoe   it's very stressing
here. How do you like those ink drawing. I've lost
my weight privilege my Art curio in this place is
no play here   there is three tiers here high this is
the killers of killers here   So far their just stairing
at me a Native

Gary

Hi   Good to hear from you. You sound in great mood.
Well first off here is a form of my classfication i went to
in on November   i should have a couple of letter with
information. Cusoditey - Walter said do to the serioness
of the offense they would not apply for it. I think their
supposed to send it to the prison i had it tooken from n let
them decide what to do about my good time   i applye
for how ever you spell it, to lazy to grab the dictionairy
go figure   ha! ha! This white guy name Livingston beat
my cellie up name Ira Pakota   busted his knees cap   his
ear he was bleeding out   Then there was just two of us
Indian left. this happen **6-9-01**. They try to say i was the
leader   i told them "right sure" yea, they don't kno what
their talking about. They think cause your the oldest here
you run thing's   Their stupid in my eye's. This fight started
about **7:30**AM and they pick us up about-**10** or **11**. Then
they had a fight and the restroom skaggs he admitted to
the fight, I went to see what was going on next thing i no
some white was sneaking up on me ready to hit me. I struck
out at him to get him away from me when i look down to
my left a bunch a white inmate were read to jump us. They
told them they were comeing to make sure it was **1** on **1**
bullshit   They told the cop's a bunch of shit to get their
self out of trouble   the took **6** of us to the hole   they took
230 or **270** day's of good time frome me   the rest was
10 days   **90** day's a bunch of crap. To bring this back in
their face might bring bad reactions from those people but
that's something i willing to do   take a chance to get out of
here earlyier   The man was not trying to stop it we had to
save ourselfe's from further damage on us. i don't no gary
but here is some of the paper work. i thought i sent some
paper on the fight back in **2001**   This happen at Air Way
Hight correction center or prison   who would you talk to
here the Warden or Cos Walter Skaggs paper work iam not
suppsed to have   he gave them to me hopeing i could get
my good time back.

Oh ~~XXXXXXXXXX~~ **8050106** - **C12**   can we help him
not for drugs or shit   I'am leaving soon   i think a
medium join can you please get him a $**200** where
he can get some bead's   they will take **35** percent
please   i myself will get it back   i'll probly leave most
of my bead's with him   if he has proof he bought
them he will be able to have them in get on his feet
plus with the money you send. The clothe's i ask for
just forget it, i reather see him get on his feet. you
don't even need to get me a lawyer   he's a good
young person   I've been here with him nearly a year
he never get's mail in he has never had any money just
been liveing off of me   think about it. I will never ask
you to help nobody else   he no how to bead if you do
put his name on check or money order   however you
do it   his name on money order

~~XXXXXXXXXX~~ **805010 6**-**C**-**12**
~~XXXXXXXXXX~~
~~XXXXXXXXXX~~
~~XXXXXXXXX~~A **99109**
put it like to him but from his mom or they will not
except the check here   well i hope you like the
drawing + moccinson   I feel my time getting short
and i don't know what i'am going to do when i get out
I've been thinking about my freedom alot lately   I try
to stay busy   well i'am in my cell by beading   i don't
draw much   My cellies's dont quite under stand don't
toch my drawing or flick their wet hair around get stuff
on picture   irritate's me when they keep looking over
my shoulder ha! ha! That's why i don't draw much
here. i guess i'am just getting old   I'll call you saterday
after noon ok or night. I shall close for now ok   be
good   please think about the help for him. I shell
right you later   take care   Still no post card ha! ha!
you beat the post card back

Gary

Hi. I don't no what to say   There is not much going on here
same old prison shit   Just trying to keep my mind occipied.
So are you going to be able to help him out or not. You
said you would send me some money   you don't half to
send me the money, just send it to Arron   I wrote you and
a letter how to do it, if not what can i say   I'am just sitting
here stressing. Forget the lawyer i was involved in a fight
in their   Not going to let me out when their supposed to
Fuck it. It would be a waste of money to get a lawyer. Life
a bitch in here they got us lock up tight when i go to the
yard, or shower, ice, work they make us line up in shake us
down cause of the stabbing crazy   They say he die   i don't
no Tho. You have any new picture   if you do send some if
you can. Are you ok or what? How did your visit go with
your Mother   Fine i hope   They will probly be moveing me
to a medium facility comeing up April **5** is it   i try to rember
it but keep forgetting   how old will you be   **54** yea or nea.
Well ill close for now   later Gary
Martin Cothren

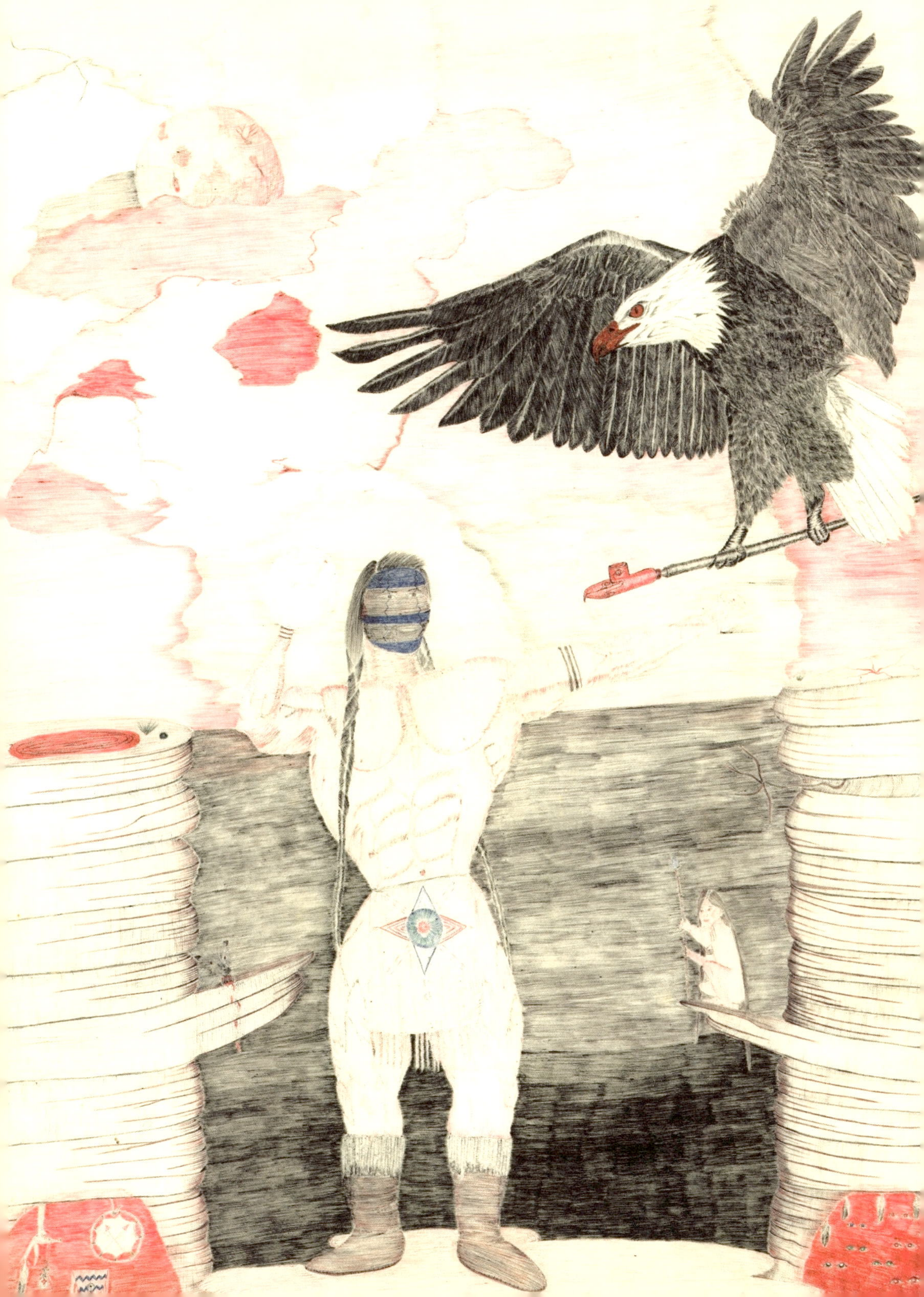

After an anxious 3-4-hour drive to Walla Walla, I picked him up from the State Penitentiary. He wasn't particularly talkative, almost as if he couldn't talk. They gave him a plastic bag with his belongings but he wasn't smiling; he wasn't about to give an inch to the scum that held him down for eight long years. As we literally walked through the last gate to freedom, he still exhibited no sign of emotion or kept it well hidden. We drove a bit and stopped at some nondescript diner wherein he inhaled the equivalent of a "last meal." Next stop—some cheap mall on a commercial spine just outside Yakima. He moved about the aisles like a caged animal. The brightness of the florescent lights made him visibly agitated. Later there would be money issues surely to arise with the free man but this was not the time. Nevertheless, I was uncomfortable handing the cashier my credit card as Martin hovered nearby. After buying him a pair of everything and a coat, we had one more stop to make. He wanted to see his son, who lived with his mother on the res. Once we arrived, knocked on the door and exchanged pleasantries, at least with his ex, the scene grew quietly intense. Very few words were spoken. His son had an ankle monitor on for dealing drugs. I won't say that the fruit doesn't fall far from the tree. Martin tried to give him a finely made beaded feather he had crafted in prison. The boy would have none of it and went back inside, without even acknowledging Martin's presence. One couldn't really

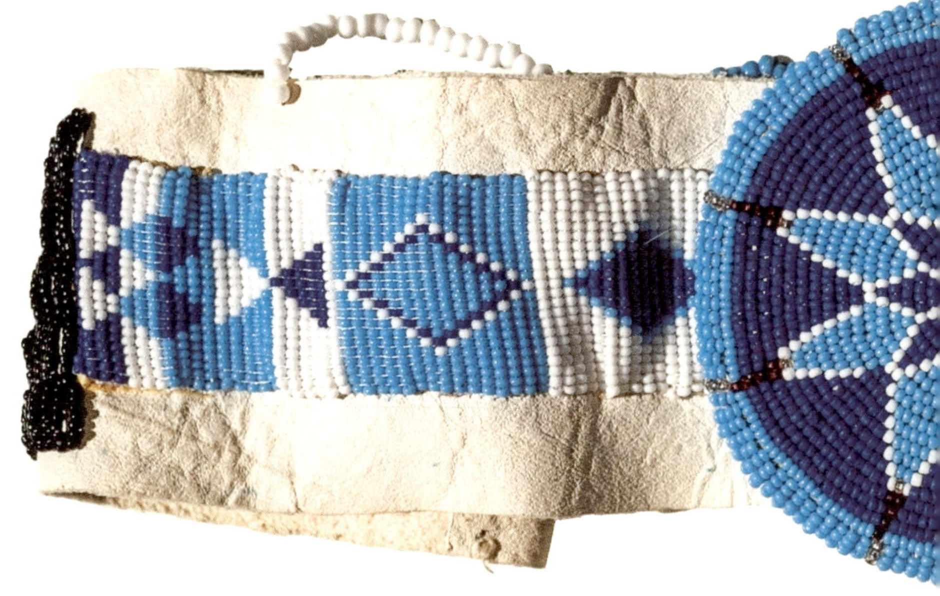

blame him but I could see it pained Martin deeply. This would possibly be his last connection to the tribe and the last time he would ever see any of his family. Soon we were on our way back to Seattle.

I decided in my own mind I could, should, would have Martin stay with us for a week knowing what happens after that was anybody's guess. I couldn't even face it. Would I just ask him to leave, throw him out, give him keys! What? I decided not to think about it. That first night we welcomed Martin "home" with a salmon dinner and a couple bottles of wine. Finally relaxed, we conversed looking at pictures and catching up on our respective lives.

We drifted into a friendly political debate and out of the blue an unfortunate, very unfortunate misunderstanding brought up the dark and very painful history of Native Americans. Everything got heavy. Surely the wine had much to do with it but it didn't matter. I had to calm Martin down or all hell was going to break loose. I feared for my family but tried to ride it out realizing, fuck, I don't know this person really...or do I? "Come on Martin, we are not the enemy, man!" I understood right then, there was no way I could conjure enough empathy that would be satisfactory. We all crashed but I couldn't sleep; I was wide awake thinking about the next day.

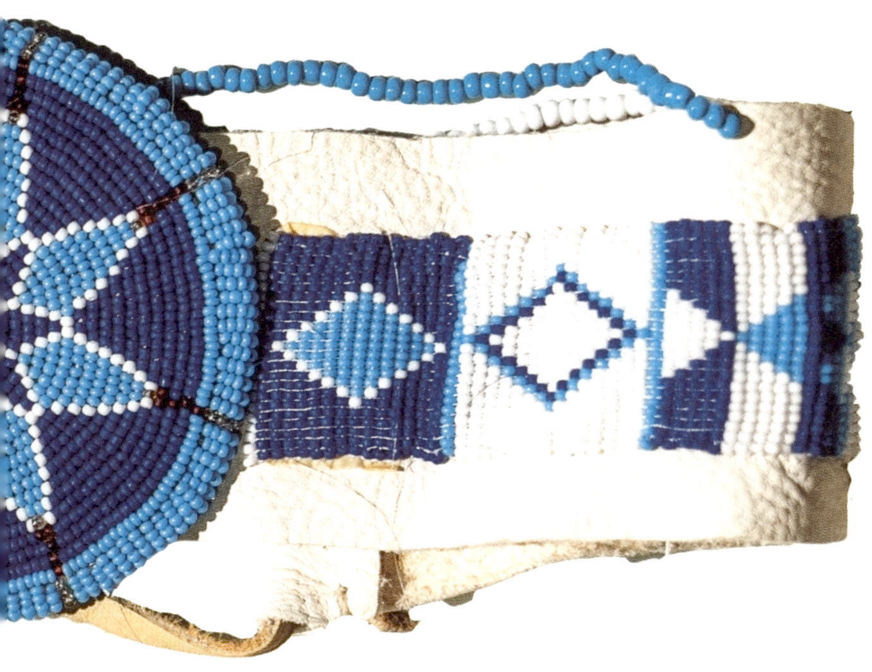

So how is your wife doing   And your daughter doing **2**,
well and school. tell your daughter i said thank you for
tapeing the music on the littel I pod   I trying to locate my
money right now, I'am tap for my money   Can i borrow
$**40**. in cash no check's here, but i can have a check
here, but they allowed cash in the mail, please n they will
give me the cash right away   I should have two check's
comeing to you on the Dec   You can take the money
the $**40** from the check that i have comeing there. I try
not to borrow money from you or Disturb you   I've been
lockup **27** days already   I relly have no contact out there
everybody has cell phone's and have on the move. It
was **5°** below **0** zero the last **2** night's wish i was there to
enjoy   I have **6** sleeping bags **7** or **8** blanket's a four men
tent. And a wild red and **4** black feet ~~coyote~~ fox that hangs
out at our camp. It's a ~~relly~~ real cool ~~coo~~ fox. I'am sitting
here stairing out my window enjoying what freedom i can
see from the window. Fog is in now, so what in the fog is
comeing down n sticking to the tree's   Look's pretty kool
turning everything white. I don't kno what they are going
to do to me. It is **5:00**pm and it is dark already   I'am
trying to rember when my frind die Joe the twin the one
i would drink with   one of the twin's the one i help bring
back his grocery   He die in the summer brain Hemoriage
from Alcolhol   They flew him home to his family   Some
island Barrow or Bethel, A couple week's After the cops
gave us a notice to move out or they would burn or
tear down our tent   we stay for **3** more weeks then we
moved, he went his way about **10** mile's down the road
to far for me so i went and found another aera to camp.
It was a nice summer hear   Spent my time checking out
the surrounding. Fishing, panning gold, tracking old Black
bear track's   I must close this letter for now   you take
care   I will write more to you! Take care my frind
Martin Cothren

From time to time, my daughter and I would send Martin
music, anything to help keep him occupied. It wasn't always easy,
depending on the rules of the particular pen and more likely the
whims of the guards. He was fond of reggae and his own tribe's
drumming and chant music. The strange bedfellow was his lure
to Dylan's, *John Wesley Harding* which he would play repeatedly.
Lots of repetition and counting in prison—a kind of involuntary
meditation that helps pass the time. On the phone he sometimes
sang—it was always "Drifter's Escape," and I would come right
back at him with "The Ballad of Frankie Lee and Judas Priest,"
even though I can't sing worth a rat's ass. He mentioned the
Indians on the album cover, perhaps unbeknownst to him, or it
didn't matter, they were Indians from the east.

For several months Martin tried helplessly to get himself
together. Couldn't hold a job; was getting drunk and doing drugs
consistently. I knew it wouldn't be long before he'd get busted
for something and that the smallest crime would no doubt send
him back for a disproportional amount of time. I wanted to help
him and at the same time anger was building up inside me. This is
when I'd have to zoom out and see that it would take a miracle for
this life to change fundamentally. I came up with a plan, somewhat
out of desperation to get him to Alaska where he could hopefully
land a fishing job and break the vicious cycle that had kept him
down all his life. This was the only real possibility, knowing he still
had a hankering for fishing and that he could make real money
doing it. Once airborne, I had to admit I felt relieved. My wife was
afraid of him and I was too at times. Anytime he 'd been drinking
his mind could turn on a dime and suddenly I was a member of
the genocide society. Now he and I would be at a safe distance.

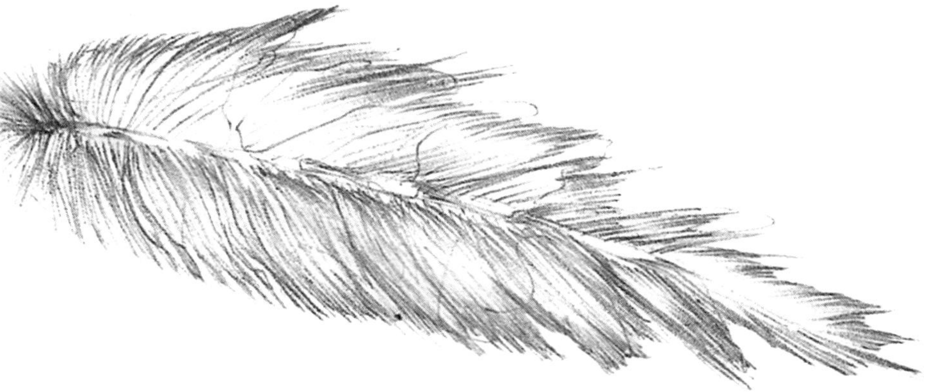

I can't believe they never sent your letter back.
STRIKE **1** for the good guy's told you ~~to~~ they be
takeing stuff here. So how is your family.   Did your
Daughter get her book back? or Did they take that
two. Today is Thursday Veterans Day   no snow
Lockdown for **5:30** count in the evening   today is
Friday   It's been a long week have not been hear
a week yet   it **10 00**AM   I did **50** pull up since
I've been hear **10** at a time yea! for the dummy.
They serve breakfast at **6:30** lunch at **11:20** Dinner
at **5:00** plastic cutlery. It's starting to snow or rain
can't tell. [   ] **5.00** thinking about about being at
my moms house when i was **12** yr old   cold out but
warm in my parent's home smokeing a cigg outside
with a frind of mine name Carl ~~Morgan~~ next to the
chimely   My mom called it the oakwood house
because the house was surround by oakwood
trees + was built out of oak plus all the furniture
was oak. Summer was beautiful there. Used to go
on vacation to Kansas City, Kansas plus the Ozarks
then to Arkansas. Most of my family live up in the
mountains alot cold in these cells. I have a lump
the size of a egg in my leg on top of my musle ^{thigh}
muscle. It been starting to grow again.   i might
go get it check out sometime it hurt's sometime
not the lump the muscle around the aera   people
are dying to get out n i keep getting lockup fuck
up   It's **4:15** people getting ready for chow. I'am
hungry   I was out with this pretty good looking
Alaskan woman. She told me she was ^{I'am} horney ha!
ha! well I better let you go   later   Gary. Thank you
for the help   Tell your daughter + woman i said hi
plus Rain [Rayne]

                    down in out
                         The wall
                         Pink Floyd

Charges Filed
Sep. 25, 2006
Charges/Offenses
Assault 3 - Cause Fear of Injury W/ Weapon | Misc./Weapons 3 - Felon in
Possession | Malicious Destruct Property - Not Own | 5aac75.022 (C):
Attempt to Snag or Failure to Release Snagged Fish - Freshwater | 5aac75.022
(A) (1): Using Fixed or Weighted Hook - Freshwater | Operating Under The
Influence | Trespass - Business/Commercial Property | 49cfr392.16: Seat
Belt Must Be Used If Installed (17aac25.210) | Fgc78 - 929 (B) (3): Insurance
or Other Security in Effect | Amc8.35.410: Intoxicated Person on Roadway |
Amc8.35.400: Consuming Alcohol in a Public Place

Source
Administrative Office of Courts (Alaska)

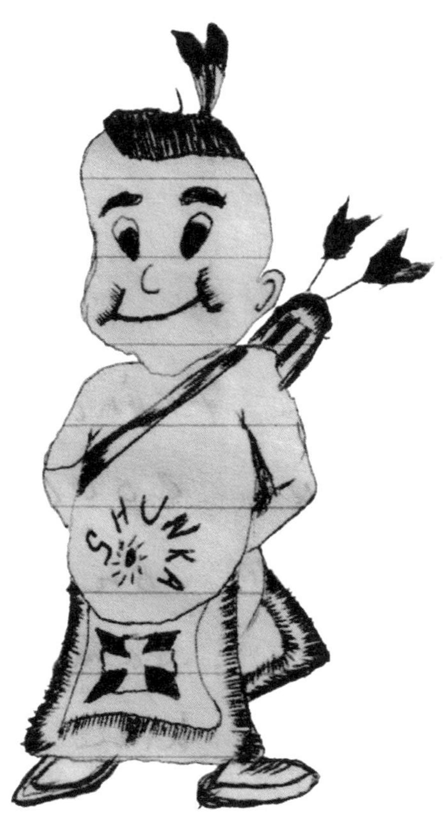

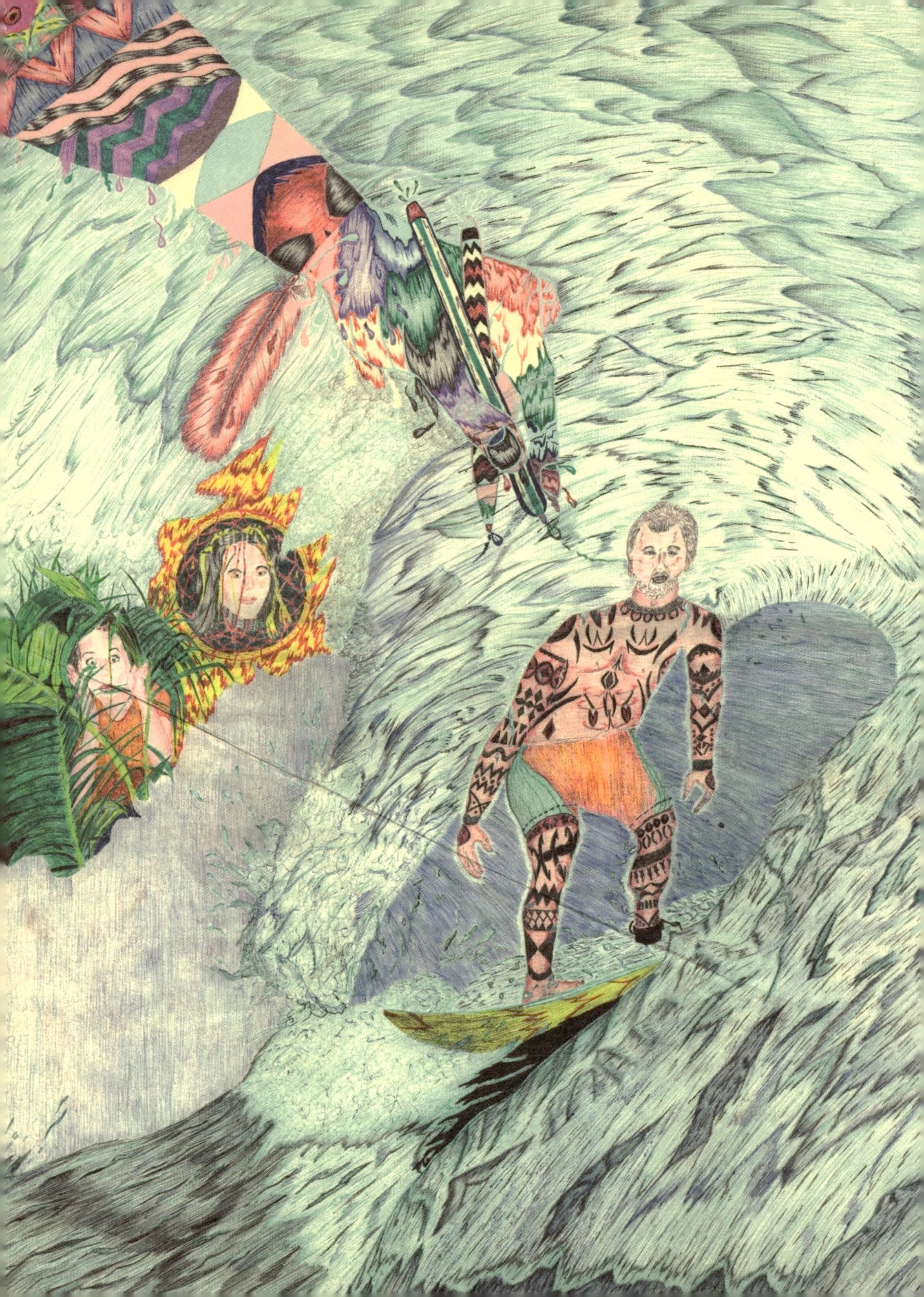

On occasion we had long anecdotal talks about art, drugs, fishing, beading and even surfing—he was eager to give it a try but we never got around to it between his jail times. I frequently wondered if any real connection was developing between us. But for God's sake, what was it—what could it possibly be? Eventually, I accepted I could never know the meaning of whatever it was and took it as it came. To some I was being used at every turn by a typical con. And yet there were too many meaningful exchanges for me to know I wasn't being played. We both knew our origins and that the consequential paths we'd taken were profoundly different. Obviously, the socio-economic gap between us stands out, but getting more down to earth he was an out and out street person with the smarts to match. When he elected to receive five-thousand dollars in compensation for a fishing accident (instead of turning it down, getting some legal help and in all likelihood getting a much bigger payout), I was distraught; I was stuck in the mud of common sense—more to the point, my perspective was what the right mind of a "civilized" person would do. But Martin lived NOW— and by *now* I don't just mean one day to the next in terms of paying the bills, but on the razor's edge in survival terms. He had no choice. His *now* wreaked havoc somewhere in Zeno's paradoxes. Perhaps unconsciously I wanted him to score big time so he could finally pull himself out of the circular madness and live above the bottom line and not "bother" me. And yet, even this far into it I couldn't imagine divorcing myself from this strange relationship—one that was certainly like no other I'd ever had.

At some point I gave Martin an Indian head half-ounce gold piece. It was from the early 1900s; the new Buffalos hadn't become available yet. I thought of it as a good luck piece as I tried to separate our lives... It didn't take long before he "lost it." chances are it simply became fodder for another drink or toke with whoever happened to be present.

I went through a "gold bug" period that lasted about ten years. It would be dishonest to suggest I didn't still have a foot in that door. My most obsessed period coincided with Martin's longest prison time. At one point, I had accumulated a substantial amount of gold and silver, both in numerous denominations and adorned with a plethora of images, most notably with animals—dragons, eagles, pandas, kangaroos and cats among others. And then there is Lady Liberty who graces coins across the entire precious metal spectrum, but I digress. When you have that kind of stash in your house one can't help but feel like an outlaw, let alone be paranoid. This was the time I came closest to buying a gun or two. It was one of those details that I stupidly told Martin about, and of course, I immediately regretted it. At the same time, I realized I didn't trust the Indian as one would a good friend, and that simply brought me down. Through the years he would sometimes needle me about it, knowing that I'd get a little agitated. I had meticulously hidden my coins and bars in various places throughout my bunkerlike studio, some "in plain sight." In other words, for the person looking, "no one would hide it there." There are of course those that would follow up with "or would they?" A friend of a friend (or was it a friend of a friend of a friend?) enthused about the theory as I was packing my bags to head back to the states one day from The Netherlands...with about 50 hits of LSD. Even though Martin was usually at a safe distance, I was relieved after I had sold a good chunk of my gold and paid off my mortgage—the barbaric relic had done me good.

Gary

Hello! How's it going?? way up younder in the Europiean hillis
how ever you spell it. Ha! Ha! I called your not around   talk to
your daughter for a few minute   none of my junk got there yet.
It' about **6:30 6:40** AM. Decided to write you. I liveing with
2 young white Indian's and a perverted old Indian that's **52**
yr's old in alway in trouble raiseing hell with the cops   Alway's
talking to this young Indian, "back in the day's" Id would of
knock you out in suck your cock soma perverted story over and
over   we told him you got to move he's no good, bitches about
his aera bitches about the rock roll music call's it fag music   once
to watch cowboy music all the time. He evan shaves his bed
sheet every night   say the fur ball's drive him crazy, I don't think
he half's to worry about fur ball's driveing him crazy   he's as
Looney as you can get. The old guy has **25** years in already   he
finish one life sentence already   now he has to start another.
He is wacko! So where is my letter from younder. Can't draw
Can't bead in this cell   guy driven us crazy. Did you get my
picture's   The surfer is your's   hope you like it   Don't work with
color pen's much   hope you like it   I sent other not done just
toss those   their no good. Thank you for christmas + New Year
money   it was needed. Yes iam getting short on time   be shorter
if they gave back my good time   they did not evan send it to the
Warden to check out   They said they ned to investigate it. I ask
them what do i **1/2** too do call a Lawyer in they said yes. Fucked
up place   forgive the cussin there   Everybody in that fight lost
30 90 day they took from me mass day   i don't no it i sent you
the paper work on that time. Well you no me i'am in need of a
few buck's   can you help. Sure wish i could get work release or
something   **18** mon'th left come fab. I hope i get out before i
die   I have a basketball game tonight   nearly got in a fight last
game   crazy. I shell close for now   Take care   Write me   Send
me pictures please
        Later My Friend

                How your women doing?
                Ha! Ha!

During my obsession with gold I managed to
create a couple of works exploring the meaning,
metaphors and "value" of gold. For *Frustrum*, I
created an animation of an eagle caught in a pylon
flapping its wings against the electrical wires, the
overseer of a bullion bar of gold debossed with
the tag, "For everything which is visible is a copy
of that which is hidden." The 426-ounce bar was
mounted dead center in a pool of petroleum
reflecting the eagle's every move. At times, it was
uncanny how the work conjured up Martin's
overall predicament. He had sent me a number
of drawings with eagles that perhaps were doing
flybys in my subconscious. A lesser known fact is
that Native American Indians, sometimes referred
to as the Mississippians built mounds reminiscent
of pyramids that retained the frust(r)um like
structure.

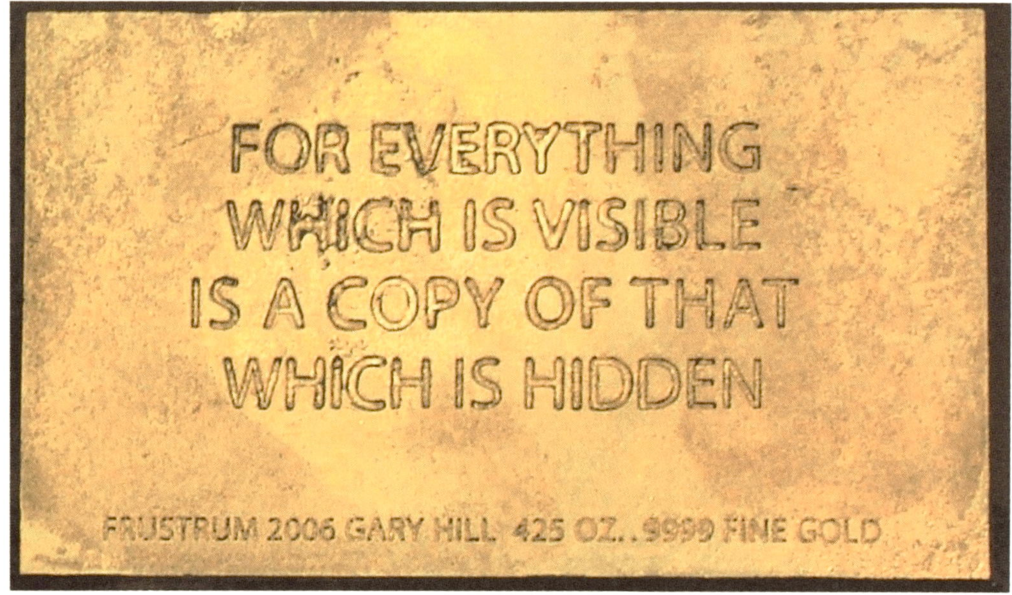

Gary Hill, *Frustrum* (detail), 2006. Collection Foundation Cartier, Paris, France

Martin Cothren (martincothren@yahoo.com)
Fri, Oct 28, 2005 11:26 am
To: you Details

gary hello how are you doing ? it was nice to hear from you. i,am trying to figure out how to youse this computer right now in i still can not spell correctaly ha; ha; hello magdalucca how are you doing? life is very exciteing.in very amazeing i have not lost my mind yet gary they offer me job in alaska but as i told you i.am not a clean sole my journey to alaska was very fun evan in hard times something i.ll alwas i will rember thanks for the help i got the cob web out of my mind a little bit of life has come back to me .i watch a moose come into the city every body ran they have this wall around mulldoon to keep the bear out of the houseing aera iseen one eagle the hoe time i was there i met this this indian sister up there she was a knock out . you people should go to alaska in check it out it,should be good for you . go be a speaker or put on a show up there or show a peace of film of me in northpole where they would not cash my checks from you i should let you go for now later my friend good bye magdalucca

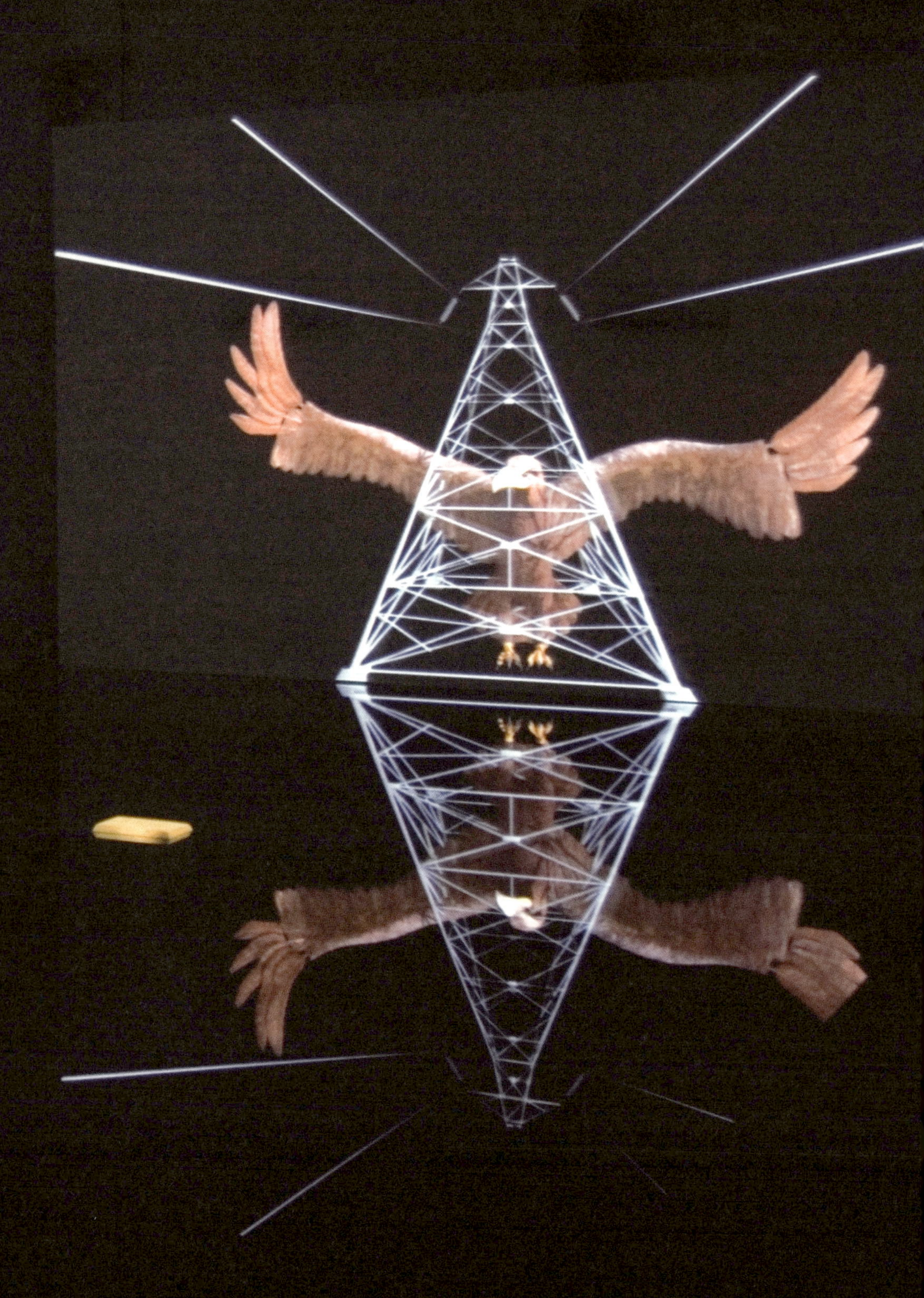

Tomorrow is the **1**st   I work last winter for **3** month
cleaning a house for a Insurance company, chipping ice
scooping snow out the house takeing Inventory   it was
a grueling hard job, freezing always if it was **10°** to **20°**
zero^{below}   it was always **10°** **15°** degrees more.   I would
^{make} $**700** $**800** a week   **3000**$ a month in cash, under
the tabel table. What ever is correct. Met a couple this
summer. They introduce me to a frind of theirs and they
took me to the moutain to their frind's cabin. We stay **3**
days went gold panning, He the old men that new the Aera
was showing me about panning gold   seems easy but it's
not. I did not get to see the wolf But they got to see a wolf
my frind's did. I was looking some where else. We left all
the Rifels at the cabin. There was on this trip, just scouting
for a spot to pan   we had a detector device with us found
more without it. He had a old fire stove + his house that
is how we kept warm   in the mourning had to go get our
water from the lake   Fresh water but we still had to boil it
to take a bath or to have drinking water or shave etc! etc!
Evan had a old out house we had to use   Quite freakish
in the middle of the nite, i figure you get so use to the city
life you forget what living in the wood's is about, diffrent
sound's smell thing's that go creak in the nite or day time.
I need to kno if you can pick me up a pair of kool wire rim
reading glasses in send them to me before the **18** of Dec
That is when i go to sentanace

                        I will write later my frind
                                Take care
                                How your wife Magna

Gary Hill, *Frustrum*, 2006. Collection Foundation Cartier, Paris, France
Photo: Patrick Gries

30 30 NOV **12:30**
Hello Gary It was good to hear from you   Sorry about
your Thanksgiving   Glad Every thing turn out for you
then   I thought that is when your family is supposed to be
together   So your women is a practicing [little drawing
of a Buddha] ha! ha! I was just reading a book or magazin
brouseing really threw it first time i listend to news **2** day's
ago i did not even no Korea Bomb South that's how much
i'm out of contact with the world right-now   I'am about
to go outside They moved me from h^EMA mod to another
mod its **1/2** and **1/2** it's a pill mod, where disturb inmates
on medication stay   They have a over flow here so they
move **4** of us from the intake unit to this one   Now i think
about the book your daughter sent me called One Flew
Over the KK nest. So I'am back in the cell   They lock us
down early   Watch them bring some guy by me in a
wheel chair   So I'am sitting in this cell watch my pen work
out a letter to you   It's cold out   went to the Gym in work
out tonight   just got back it a pretty good size prison
Gym   Dreading this trip to Colorado   Trying to draw a
christmas card. So today is the **2** Dec **11:30**AM We had
no yard this mourning So back to the wheelchair victium
he try to kill hisself or hang his self on his bunkbed ladder
Their so small some of these Eskimo they can do that   I
was watching this one little Eskimo he had to clime up
on his toilet spread his leg and put his other foot on his
bunk just to look and the mirror   That's how close the
toilet bowl is to the bunk. my lovely abode in the wall
[drawings]
Later Gary Merry Christmas   send me some picture's.
Dreary in my cell   no polaroid

BO 30 Nov 12:30

Hello Gary It was good to hear from you Sorry about your Thanksgiving Glad Every thing turn out For you the I thought that is when your Family is supposed to be together. So your women is a practicing 🌼 ha! ha! I was just reading a book or magazin browseing really threw it. First time. I listend to News 2 day's ago I did not even no Korea Bomb south that's how much i'm out ot contact with the world right now I am about to go outside They moved me From ENA mod to another mod it's ½ and ½ it's a pill mod where disturb immate's on medication stay They have a over Flow here so they move 4 of us From the Snake unit to this one Now i think about the book your daughter Sent me called one Flow over the K K nest. So I am back in the cell They Lock us down early. Watch them bring some guy back by me in a wheel chair So i am sitting in this cell watch my pen Work out a letter to you It's cold out went to the Gym in work out tonight just got back it a pretty good size prison Gym Dreading this trip to Colorado Trying to draw a christmas card. So Today is the 2 Dec 11:30 AM We had no yord this Mourning So Back to the wheel chair Victium he try to Kill hisself or hang hisself on his bunkbed ladder Their so small some of these Eskimo they can do that I was watching this one little eskimo he had to climb up on his toilet spread his leg and put his other Foot on his bunk just to Look and the Mirror. That's how close the toilet bowl is to the Bunk.   my Lovely Abode in the wall

Dear   Later
                                        Gary
                                        Merry
                                        Christmas
                                        Send me
                                        some picture's
                                        dreary in my
                                        Cell
                                        No poloroid

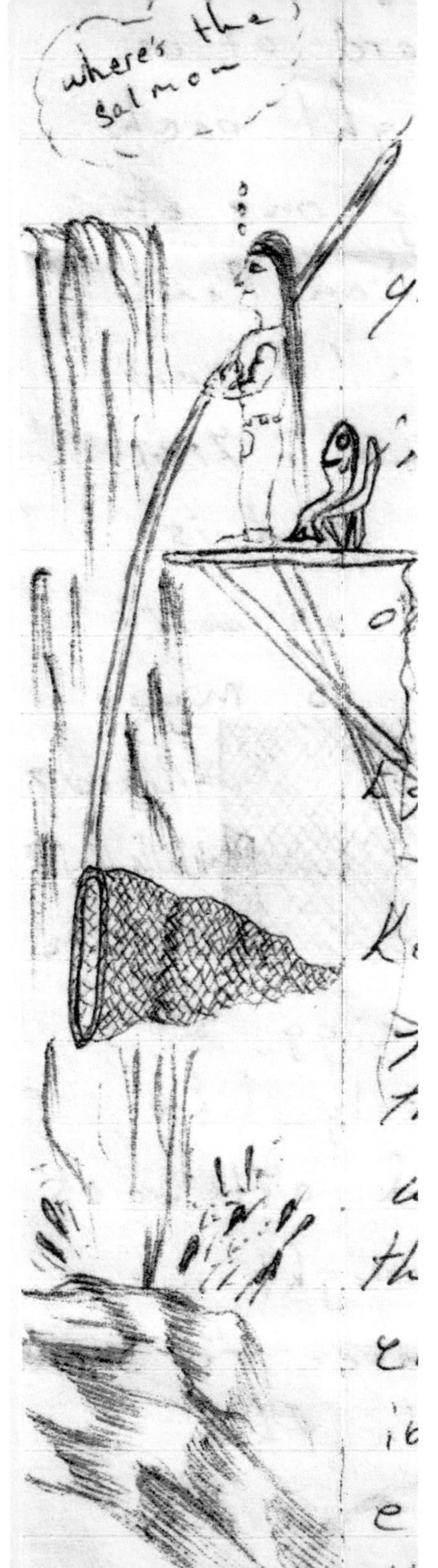

I must have said goodbye a half dozen times—
seeing him off to Alaska, kicking him out of my
house or simply going our separate ways after
meeting on the street and exchanging a few terse
words. Even while he was in Alaska, following
a request for some cash, I wrote a note in bogus
legalese that I made him sign before securing him
a hotel room for a few nights—something along
the lines that he would never ask for money again.
Who was I kidding? In the end I sent him three
times to Alaska with additional trips to Dutch
Harbor, Juneau and Ketchikan hoping again for
that elusive fishing gig that would miraculously
turn everything around.

Gary

How Are you doing? I hope this letter find you + your family
in good health. were lock down again   thrown   back in our
cells. No showers or clean clothes for **3** day   last time it was
for **6** days one shower in **6** day crazy   They feed Breakfast at
10:00 or **10:30** AM   lunch at **3** or **4** pm afternoon supper
about **9 930** at nite crazy   They just sit up there doing nothng
like us   They have this lady cop that really like looking at
naked men when they give us shower she is right there running
up n down the tier trying to catch a look she trys to act like
she isn't looking. Stupid place   This place is mostly Indian so
they think every body is stupid here   They have no emergency
button in the cell in case your dying or haveing a heart attack
or getting your ass beat down their very slow here   it's **630**
i'am eating a bowl of top Ramen I'am lucky to have some food
in my locker else i would be hungry as hell   They got a lot
of big spider starting to come in this prison cell block   I'am
writing you in parcaly light they wont even turn on the little lite
or nite lite where we can read or write   I guess this is Broke
back mountain territory   So today is [?] **17** We got let off
lock down on the **14** end the afternoon got out on Thursday
2 [?] on since i talk to you on the phone. It's supposed to be
tornado season here i think. I saw a Bunch of eskimo standing
at the fence looking at a open field   i ask them what they were
watching they told me their looking for cowboy out in the
open field   Makes since i guess lot of these people come from
small neighbor hood island and Alaska in always see cowboy
in Colorado   Well i no i need money when i get out   i need
one more check for a pair of tennis shoes plus money to send
out stuff when i leave here **5** more months   No package yet
probly cause of lockdown   how is Crystell doing + her son is
he still sick   Well i will close for now   how is your daughter
doing on her walk about threw Mexico?? Later Bro Take Care

P.S. Will let you kno when beads are here
Received my birthday **5-16-11**package
thank you very much

Today it is cold out. Just went outside n did a garbage run took **5**
minutes. Freezing out trying to look or think positive
I was just thinking, I never did get to see the video with me in
it the viewing. Sort of made me think it's sort of like my driking,
thing's   i   have missed in my life black out a peace of my life
missing.   Just got back from working out waiting for count,
it's very exciteing doing count here [little drawing] what hair
is left Ha! Ha! How are you really doing it's six A.M. looking at
the street light in the mourning darkness same at nite watching
thing that could disapear relly quick   I was out last ~~summer~~
winter listening to PaPa Roach + Mataltica me and this young
Indian woman she was Beautiful it was **20** below **0**   we went
to this place called Northway mall in grab a **1/2** gallon vodka
It's their prize drink up here. We drank with two other people
under a tree, we all had our gear on, except her, she just got
out of sleep off, she was from Fairbanks. She was **21**   I and a
frind were walking down the street going to the Liqour Store
at Northway Mall. She was walking past us   she had no winter
gear on, we ask her if she was alright, she explain to us she just
got out of sleep off the bottom of her jeans were wet from snow
she had only tennis shoes on, and a light coat. So i kept walking
behind her going to the ~~snow~~ store snow was pretty deep. Finely
i ask her if she needed another peace of clothing, I gave her
my sweat shirt to put under her coat to stay warm ask her how
about another pair of socks. I just put on a pair of clean socks **2**
pair. I always where **2** pair in the winter plus i had on my bunny
boot, she was happy she put on the other pair of socks when
we got to the Mall. We talk then we went with our frinds + drank
underneith some pine trees then we took off n went down town.
The men we was partying with was wearing a freezer suit pass
out the next day with **2-5**th vodka in freeze in the snow over nite
Crazy world up here **23** Nov that was last winter. **1** quarter mild
[mile] away from my camp a lady pass away frozen to death at
her tent **2008**# [?]. Winter are rough here if you decide to live
out in the element of the freezing tempture up here. So upon
us is another year of (old men winter hulk [?] is here. My frind
+ i went out drinking last winter after work we consume **2 5**th

vodka then went in bought **2** more fifth. That nite he broke his ankle i call the ambulance it was freezing out in snowing, I stay until the ambulance come there We started laughing because we just go done talking about alot of people walking around on cruches. He look at me and said Martin i broke my ankle and we started laughing. did not see him for **1/2** a year. During the winter on the streets its very cold so when your on the outside camping out it to cold to drink beer because they freeze with a quickness here last year they had picture of a lady throwing a hot cup coffe in the air and it froze before it hit the ground. I keep reading a sign that says welcome to Alaska. So what have you been doing. Just drinking a cup of coffee this mourning. A frind gave me a **1/2** can of coffee that was very nice jester from him. We half to order everything here from the streets. **24**th Nov. Only can food we can have, quite strange. They allow us no candy They want us to use their candy machine. Some guy left gave me his shampoh +soap + some clothes + a pair of socks. Most of my frind are street people so their always on the move. As close as they want to get near hear is when their lock up street people are quite the survivors up hear socitey does not understand that the environment is very harsh in the wintertime. Socitey + the Government + the state do not like it when people are not what they seem to be, to their way. In my eyes i've walk a long way from my family trying to chase a dream, but i've went backward in my journey. I have my window open to smell the fresh air + hear the nosiey out side a lot of planes we hear up hear. **26** Thursday. Today is Thanksgiving, very boaring in here went to sleep woke up in the room look out the window in it is snowing. Lokks like **1 1/2** inches. Not much, but it looks clean n white. th **29** day after Thankgiving it's snowing up here, I went to court they drop **4** out of **5** charges so gave me **1** charge they offer me **11** yrs now they drop it down to **3** yrs **24** suspended in do **8** month on the **8** month. So i better relly slow down on my drinking alot like give it a brake in go back to work it's still snowin out I'am watchin it come down. it's about **11** o clock still on lockdown   It's starting to get deeper. **30** Today is the **30**, last day of Nov.

Gary
I never made it to the Parole Office   I already let them kno i am not from Alaska n i have no home here   my frind i was staying at that recived the cash it let me stay one nite and ask me to leave the next day. He was on Parole n did not want to get in trouble for haveing me there so that was ok   So i took what money i had got a place for the nite next day went back to the streets that day pick me up for hanging with some Homeless people

Now i wish i were back in Seattle more help for people that get out of jail   First time i've felt lonely   i mean lonely sort of like when my sister went back to Germany i used to go lay in her bed n hug the pillow and cry or smell the room   Lost   That is how i feel now. I livein with a men who has no family nobody to write and is dying making my day today   Do me a favor send me a picture of you + your women where i can look at some freedom faces frinds at lease i'am looking at   **3 4** yr for drinking a bottle of vodka with the homeless and i'am homeless This is insaine   They say i broke my probation by doing that   I think when you carry the box of stuff to me that day on the street corner by the coffee shop i knew my life was going backword's. I brought all i had with me from prison n hid them next to a broken down abandon box   today their still there lost articles or dreams   Tonight I traded my desserts for a cup coffee   I'am out of jail   I'am in the **1/2** half way house now. Feels Better then being in jail. I've been here **9** day's in the **1/2** house no clothes been whereing the same clothe every day. somebody lone me a pair of shorts + shirt so i went in did my laundry with the money you sent me. I'am tired of jail   all i can say is f_____!!!. Te leaves are already falling off the trees n turning gold + brown getting chilly ouside. So i have no clothes n no winter coat not looking to good Gary   I need help send me a winter coat please Their not relly helping me much in the **1/2** house for clothes and it is startin to get cold here. I'am relly and a bind   here my frind's that i kno are on Parole so their no help cant hang or get any help from them. Right now i'am trying to find somebody going out to see if they can buy me stamps n sneak them back in here

to me   They gave me **90** days here so i don't get out till the [
] **07** Oct or Nov for not reporting in the first day out plus i half
to find a place to stay. What do day expect a person with no
money to do.

I think, they think everybody has money here cause were in
Alaska. Struggle on i guess. But i keep struggling on. I came
from outside my room went n look outside n watch the leaves
blowing around on the ground, Plus falling from the trees it's
that time of the year hitting the **40° 30°** tempture already. Can
you send me picture of your trip to Russia And if my check
came send me the rest and keep what i owe you out of it thank
you just put it in between the paper again   I'am just thinking
about winter comeing on plus, Being here in Alaska for the last
5 yr and made no money this relly is sad i did not have this in
my goal's when i came here always in jail   I'am back to working
out again nothing else to do here. My frind move Tyson n
change his address, they finely rook him off of his ankel monitor
house arrest. He told me he was moveing But now i do not no
where he lives since i got lock up Plus he has to do Parole now. I
rember when i was liveing out in the wood's in a tent **30°** below
0 quite a experience that was had frost bite on my nose And my
one frind die in his tent two yr ago and a women froze to death
in our campsite. That was a rough winter being homeless n
camping out. Just sitting and trying to wake up right now   had
to take a cold pill + Ipbrofen   Starting to get sick from the cold.
Here **5.00** send to Yakama fro me need to get another ID. Cops
took my I.D. and never gave it back now that suck   So here is
5.00 Let's hope they give me another one i need that just to
get a real ID which i will do this time   when do you leave again
so here is another letter to them so can you please send them
this letter not this one the other one Ha! Ha! [little drawing-
emoji]

So if you can help me with a coat send to this place i'am at
Send cash in letter please with picture of you and Russia
Hide cash in X paper

Gary Hello!
How's it going? I hope you had a nice vacation. I'am not doing
much just kicking back being careful very thin ice up here. I don't
expect you to come n visit so that's life. But i do need your help
with the tape Their on a food strike in here started Wednesday
This place is gone Nobody eating here, food's no good here
anyway. Been trying to draw right now my drawing are slow.
Some Indians gave me some food to eat well their on strike, else
i would not have anything to eat   still no check. It's a struggle
in here for me right now I think i was better off in the hole   my
attitude sucks   stranger in a strange world around strange people
I'll send a couple of pictures as soon as i can some people are
going to give me some paper to work on Later Mister Hill Take
Care of your Self

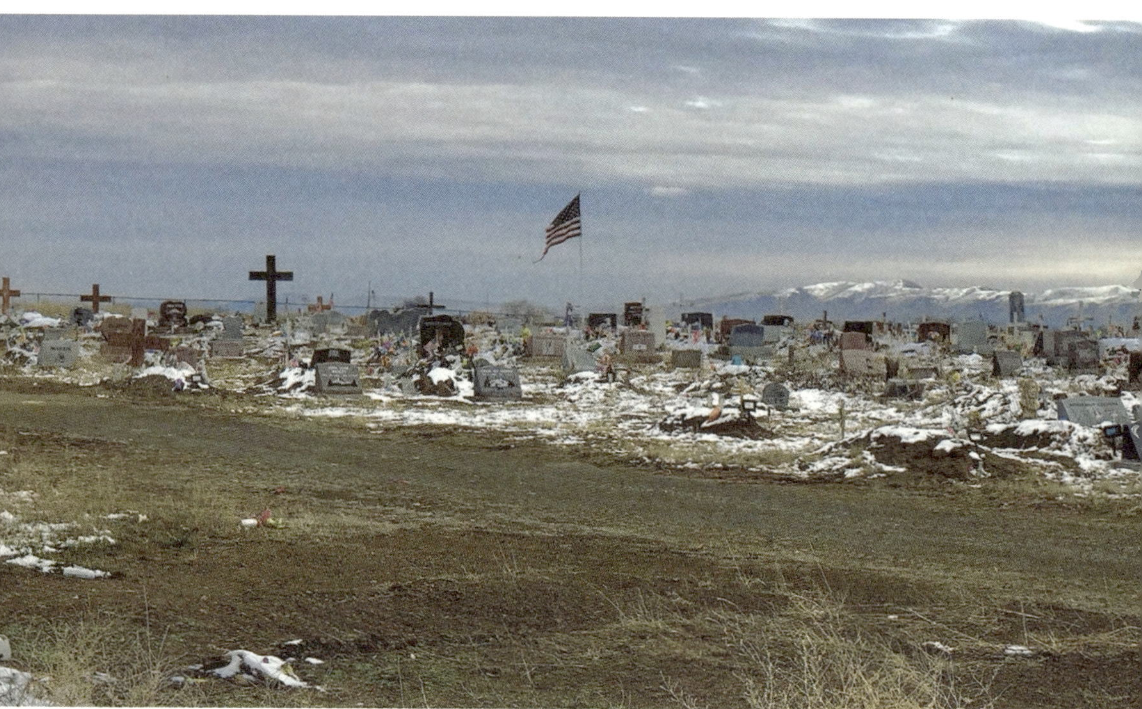

After a few years of Martin being in Alaska, I became ambivalent as to his whereabouts and what he was up to. Doing what I could for him was always checked with keeping him at arms-length. He felt his home(less) was in Seattle, meanwhile, he was held at bay far away in Anchorage. Parole boards and lack of absolutely anything kept him pinned down in the forests on the outskirts of the city, where fringe inhabitants fight to survive, steal and kill. Eventually, he returned to jail for shooting guns in the city limits. Trouble is, with a lengthy record, one little mistake, even harmless bullshit and he's back in for months up to a couple of years and that's exactly what happened over and over again. So much so I couldn't keep track. If he didn't call or write for long periods, I would wonder about him—is he in jail? Did he manage to find a way back to Seattle? Is he dead? Did I just miss his calls!?

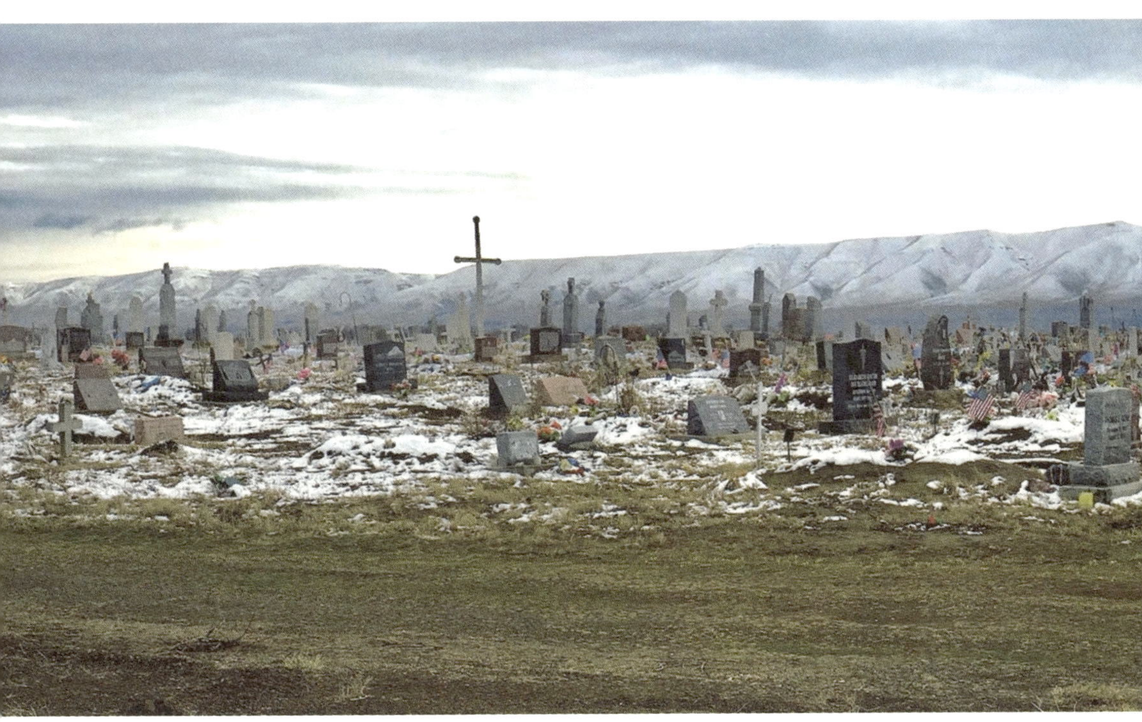

Rayne (ghstudio@hotmail.com)
To: you Details

Hi, Gary,

Martin just phoned again - he got the first
$500, but now the bondsman says
he needs to pay an additional $500 as
collateral because he is not a
resident of Alaska. He says they are
moving to sentence him this month and
he might be given 10 years.

Let me know what you want me to do.

Rayne

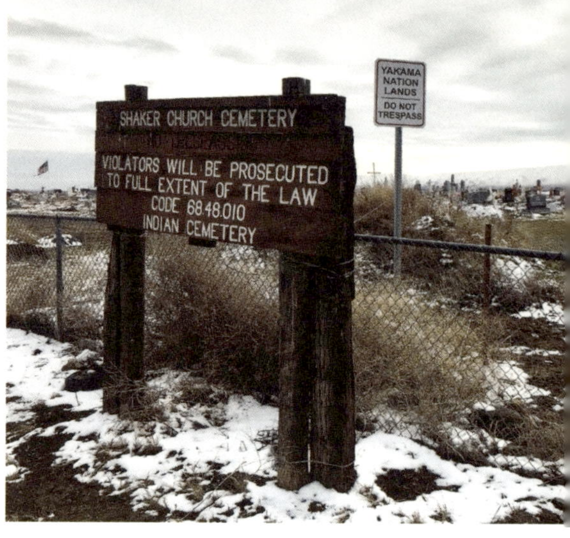

Above, below and preceding: Shaker Church Cemetery,
Yakama Nation Lands, Washington. Martin N. Cothren's
final resting place. Photos: Joseph C. Roberts

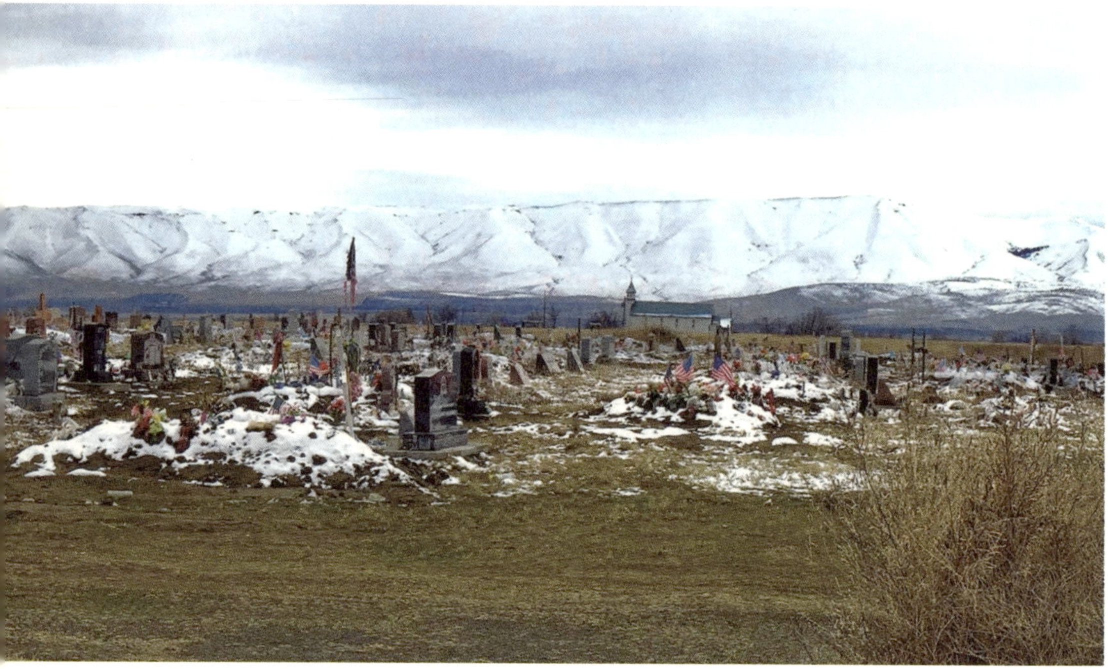

Gary

Hello! How are you   I've been trying to call you but you will not
anwser that is ok and away some bridges are just burn all up I
guess beat's the hell out of me HaHa! I'am in prison now it took
them **45** days to send me to prison that quick. A **1/2** black + Alaska
men said i punch some body but i did not cut nobody so you tell
my stupid ass i plead guiltey for no reason. Yea i don't kno Gary
i give i must do something i don't kno   They gave me **2** yrs. That
picture on the wall send me a post card of that where the lady
holding the men. I nearly shade a tear when i was sent to prison
here and now they want to send me to Arizona prison Fuck!!! Sorry
its cold and wendy here in Seward. Had to sleep with my hat + coat
on in this prison serious. Thanks for the bed and food my friend
while i was in Seattle. Never did go on that vacation together did
we so much for the dreams huh! Do you have a picture of me and
the children and you + your women   if you do sure would like
some   i don't kno what to do and nobody can help me. Like you
said You kno where I'm at and i know where you're at." I'am by
myself in this prison. i'm trying to get a hold of my ex women in
Yakima maybe you can help or not plus i need a place to send my
clothe's or they will throw then away. We half to buy all our clothes
here in prison they give us jail clothe's to where here so i will use
the money you sent me for cosmetic and some clothe's Thank for
the bond money my cellie is a white guy that's Kool   The Alaska
people don't recognized their self as Native Indian   So I relly
don't talk to them and it's a relly screw up world   I realize who i
am a Native American getting older in prison [ ] day's What kind
of alcohol was i drinking   Alaska is a Beautiful state nice scenery.
It took me all summer to see a bear i saw three of them a mother
baby + an older baby   it was wild   i went to see some friends
and they were all huddel together and their dog was standing
behind them scared of the bear   so me and a frind try to help
chase them away   didn't work my frind or associate heard a
growel from the bear and took off   no i did not make frinds with
anybody up here just work all summer drank for a couple of week's
then quit then started now i'm a drunk ha! ha! yea right!! Take care
soon as i can i will...

Mr Hill

How are you doing? & your
Family. I presently in a homeless
Transitional Facility For drunks, I am
still going in & out of the Hospital
For my Heart i now have a blood clot
on the Heart & i have one eye now
They remove it in Dec 16 2014
During a robbery on me. Ive been in
the hospital 10 to 15 times over my
Heart. I have told them to Stop
useing the affilator on me, when it
time to go its time to go. I am not
working no more not able to air. I am
supposed to get a Fake eye in Oct. They
want to do some reconstructing on my
ugly mug screws in crap like that, It is
July, in already in the 80's
summer is over They have a bunch of
whale bones here I am not happy here
Can you send a letter in 5 dollar to
Yatime for me for a federal I'd I an my
taxe appreciate it plus $5 i think got took
in the Robbery I have Kno ID Do i
any checks there if i do you can send
them to this address on the envelope i
end this letter to you

Any Book
with picture of me
in it
would be fine

Sincerly Shatter drea

Sept 4 still here
can you please send me

Mr Hill

How are you doing? & your family. I presently in a homeless transtitional
facility for drunks. I'am still going in & out of the hospital for my heart i
now have a bloodclot on the heart & i have one eye now. They remove it
in Dec 16 2014 during a robbery on me. I've been in the hospital 10 to 15
times over my heart. I have told them to stop useing the affilator [fibrillator]
on me, when it time to go it's time to go. I'am not working no more not
able no air. I'am supposed to get a fake eye in Oct. They workin to do some
reconstructing on my ugly mug screws in crap like that. It is July in already
in the 60° 65° summer is over they have a bunch of whale bone's here
I'am not happy here Can you send a letter in 5 doller to Yakima for me for
a federal ID from my tribe appriciate it plus $5 i think got tooken in the
robbery I have kno ID Do i have any check's there if i do you can send
them to this address on the envelope i end this letter to you
Any book with picture of me in it would be fine
Sept 4 still here   can you please send me what ever checks that come 1-3-
15

I'am in this stupid class call job Employment I'am doing alot of sitting
around on the street, since i can not work no more - hard time breathing
hideing at night to stay warm + safe in the winter time sleeping in emtey
car's door way parking lot emptety building being a drunk spend alot
of time in drunk tanks in the winter time to stay warm so i gut drunk every
drink just to get out of the cold no snow last year in not to cold Liveing out
of the wood's alot in doorways + panhandeling hideing in stairwells i quit
putting up my tent's people keep stealing my tent + gear so i quit owning
alot of stuff beside a gun or knife for safety As your aware i've been lock up
a view time's up here   i've been being good not breaking the law. I'am in
a enployment class witch is full of bullshit it's call job employment skills. So
I sit in these class'es in pay a game just to stay here for free. So how is your
frind in Frace doing Well my frind i will let you go. Oh yes they kick me out
for five day's last week. I'am back

Take Care
My Frind

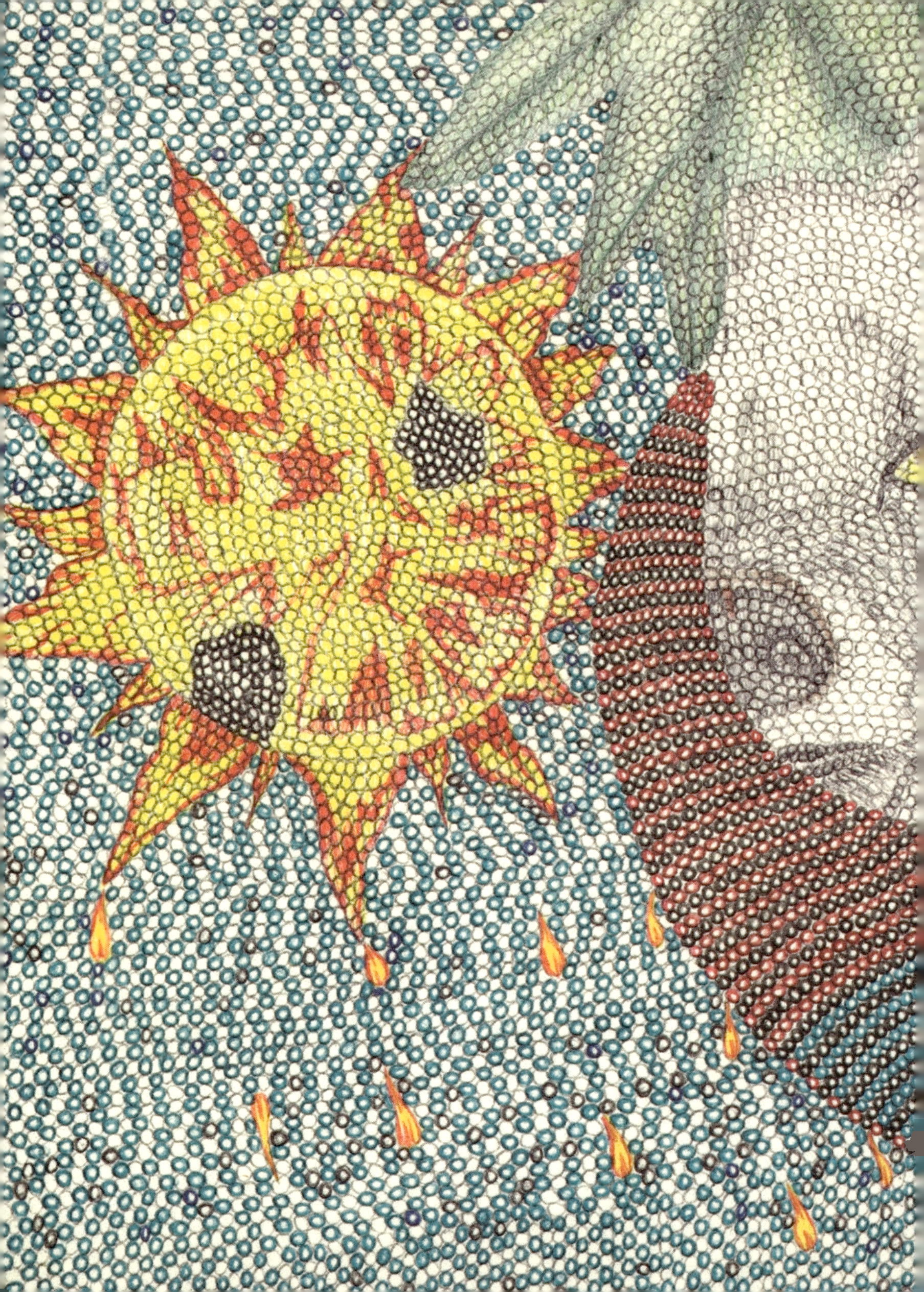

Early on Martin had authorized me as his power of attorney
allowing me to cash his monthly tribal checks, exchange them
for money orders and forward them to wherever he was. They
were usually around a hundred bucks and covered very basic
necessities. It was a pain in the ass but at some point, it was
the least I could do. After many years when, for all practical
purposes he was living in Alaska permanently, a large check
arrived in the amount of 18,000 dollars. I guess the tribe made
some considerable cash with their casino, but no matter. *Could
this be a turning point* is what flashed through my head. I sent it
to him care of a little coffee shop called bean's cafe. According
to Martin this was the safest bet. As I recall, he was staying
in a motel recovering from some heart problems at the time.
Somehow some questionable folk had gotten wind of Martin's
new found fortune and tried to force him to withdraw a large
chunk. Being Martin, with a strong sense of right and wrong
and too much honor for his own good, he wouldn't budge. They
ganged up on him and beat him so viciously that he lost an eye.

Even with 2500 miles between us, any number of associations would spark thoughts of Martin. The more time that passed, I felt I was entering a fictional domain. But his random phone calls would instantly tug me back—especially towards the end—his voice and breath barely audible, incoherent with a distinct sense of slipping away. Nevertheless, with any sustained period of no contact my imagination ran wild. Over time I slowly convinced myself that Martin needed to even the score, or at least erase anything that his forbearers might view as a compromise.

He couldn't accept seeing the gap had closed. if only slightly—too much water under the bridge—no matter the tenuous connection we had. I was the face of the race that murdered his, that annihilated all aspects of a spiritual connection. In a strange way he needed to put me down so that this inexplicable friendship might survive on a different plain of existence, more in accordance with his beliefs than mine.

I pictured several scenarios but one in particular kept repeating. He would use a shiv, one that he had slowly constructed with layers of paper, perhaps with selected skin pics from the porno mags readily available in the joint. Then out of nowhere I get a call, "Hey Gary, I'm downstairs." Even through the intercom, Martin's voice was unmistakable—gritty but soft with a slight southern drawl. I trembled, desperately trying to come up with something neutral to say. Rather than buzzing him in I went downstairs to greet him. He looked a bit older but still maintained that imposing presence. I carefully opened the gate and stepped outside keeping my distance but trying not to be obvious about it. Before I could even complete a humble salutation, in one precise move invisible to the naked eye, he shanked my gut with sheer intensity. We held eye contact (*Facing Faces*) for what seemed like an eternity. His expression was a penetrating blank stare as he pushed the blade harder and further in with a slight rotation to assure my demise. As he withdrew and pulled back, I slumped, kneeled, and finally collapsed to the ground. My eyes shifted as his image was now perpendicular. At that moment the final scene in *Last Tango in Paris* flashed through my mind—after being shot Brando steps outside on the balcony takes the gum out of his mouth and sticks it under the railing before collapsing… but that wasn't *it!* In fact, it was the cut away from a relatively long shot of his face to his POV looking across the Parisian cityscape that appeared different than before, as if he were to mutter to himself, "so this is what it's like; this is what it looks like; this is what happens." It was one of those infinite moments—the kind that are tied together on the other side… I was in a car crash:

The driver had fallen asleep before the last turn to my home after the 100-mile journey from New York City. I came to and was seemingly reviewing a film superimposed upon the very crash itself as it was taking place—time smeared. We smashed into the approaching tree in extreme slow motion and the whole scene was bathed in golden light (just like they say). As I opened my eyes and regained consciousness, I had an overwhelming urge to piss. As I reached to unbuckle the seat belt, sharp pains shot through my chest; I froze, relaxed, pissed in my pants and halfway smiled, thinking, so this is what it's like; this is what it looks like; this is what happens. I was sure I was dead, dying, or both. Needless to say, after 3 days in the ICU, I lived to tell the tale—perhaps one too many times.

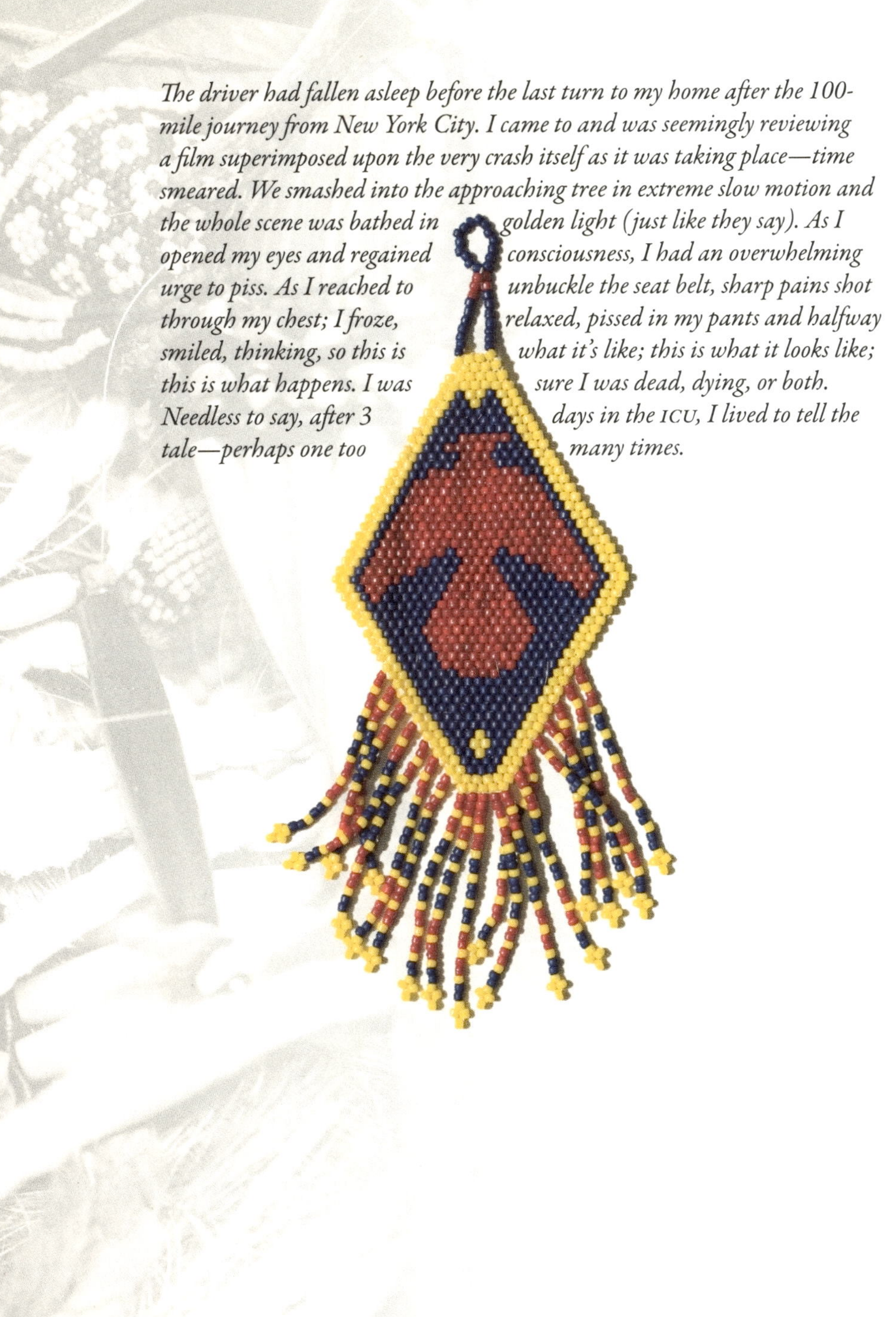

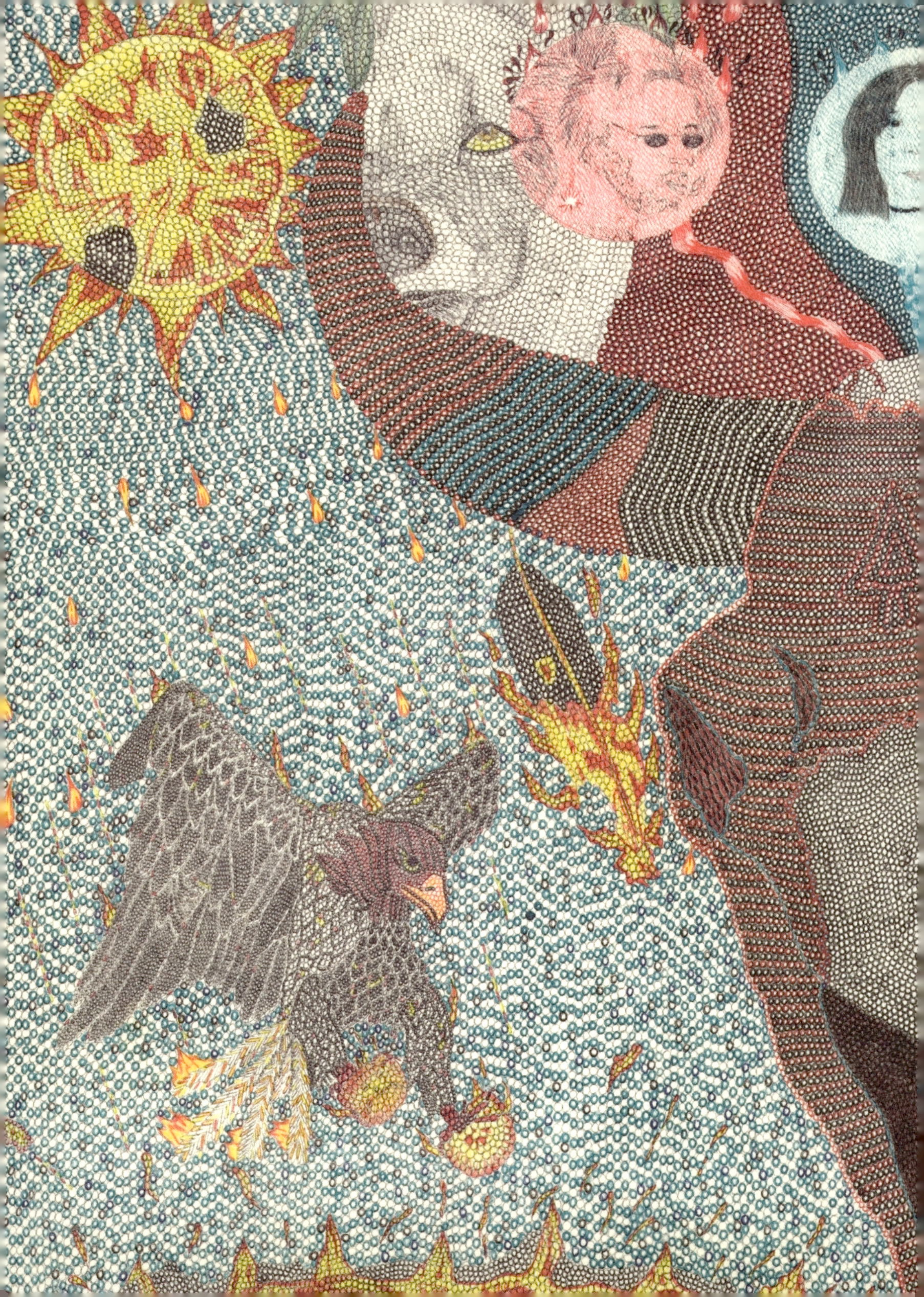

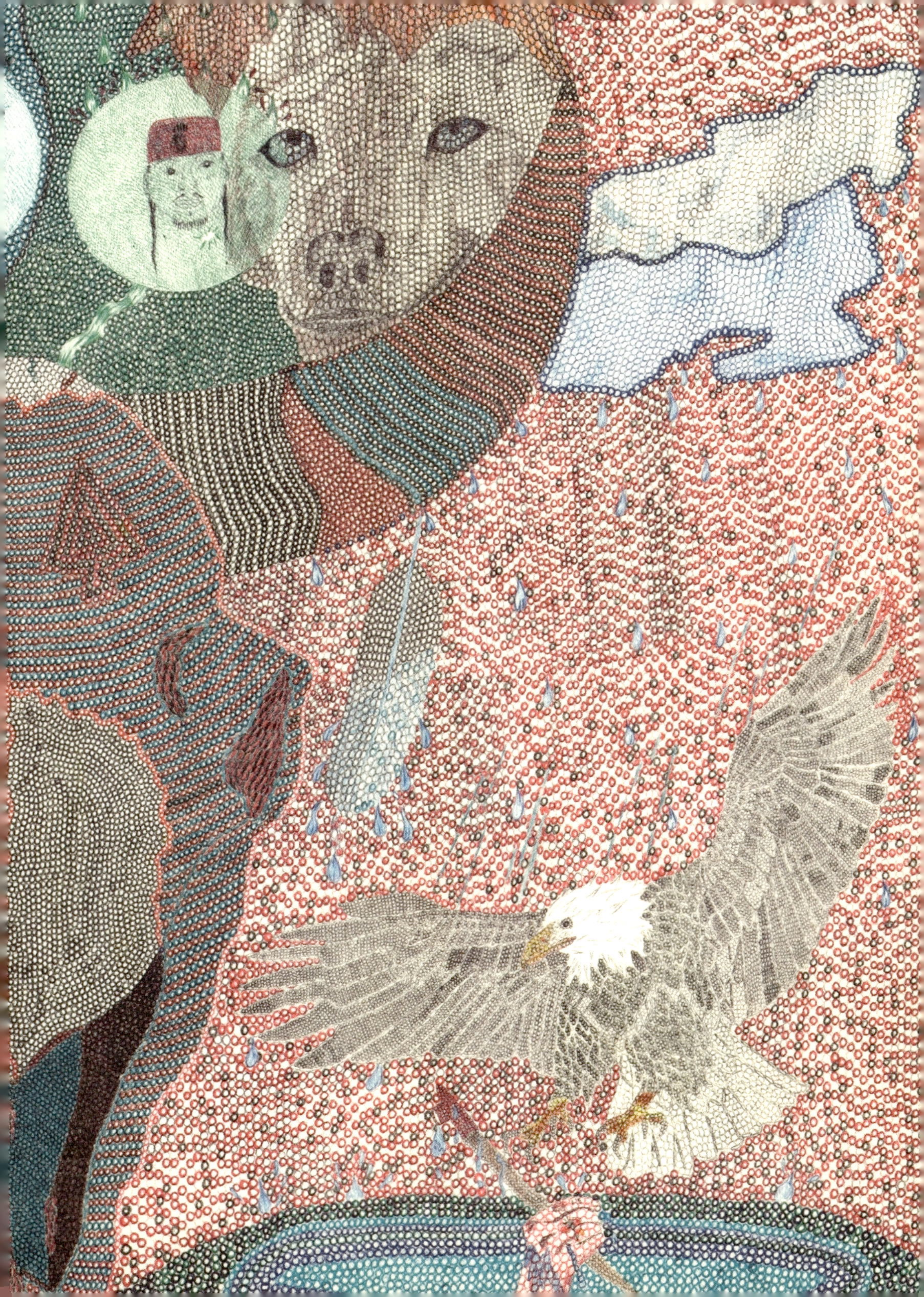

Gary   Hello!! or Hi

How are you doing   I decided i should write you a letter to let you kno I'am suspposed to get out on the **16**th of Aug. It presenty raining out   i'am going out for a walk in the rain. it doe's that alot here   rain all the time   today is th **27**th   B̶e̶e̶n̶ Ben lock down since **100** o̶c̶l̶k̶a̶ clock   who no why   They did the same thing last nite   lock down   a bunch of Lazy guard's just want to sit around and do nothing ha! ha! Crazy little prison they have here   My cellie Reading this book b Aleister Crowley   Strange book I say not to my eye's   i think i will read it tho it's out of my mind thought's. I sat and talk to this men today outside on a bench   they call him the Hammer   wack out of his mind My frind said that is why they call him the hammer   i did not ask no more   i could figue the rest out on my own   he is a lifer. Their doing ~~life~~ count right now. Were back from chow   now were lockup for count. **29**th Today it is   Just got your mail today   got up took a shower   **5**th Aug   How are you doing it's toward evenning now for us   lockup   Thinking about getting out if i'am going to make it   my cellie is waird   he's a Diabetic   he's ok. So what you been up to

I should have another check there i hope. I need to find a place to stay when i get out   i get out Monday **16**th Aug   i will need it. So what did you think of Russia   I'am sick of Alaska in another hard winter comeing up   last year it got

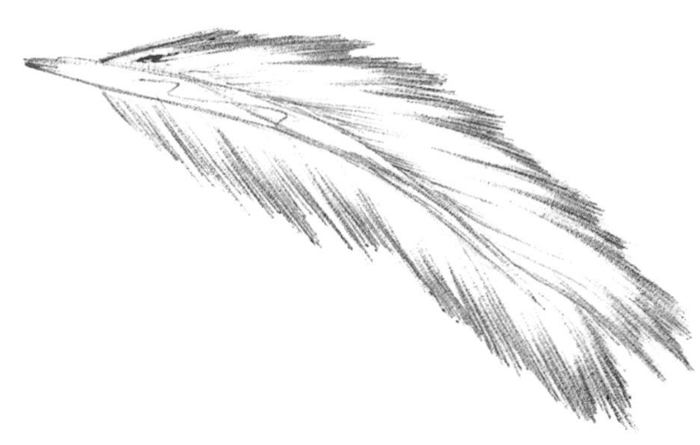

cold in Sept. It's been rainging alot up
hear in were right on the bay realy   in all
it doe's is rain   sick of it like prison. What
you can do is wired money if it's there in
i'll pick it up when i get to Anchorage on
Monday. Today is Friday the **6**th **12:00**
clock   I i got to yard in work out for a
hour or two   My righ shoulder mess up
I'am worry about a place to stay when i
get out   They can send me back or have
me lock up if i don't find a place to stay
when i get out   I could stay in the mission
but no thank's   that is where this men in
his family hang out when i first went to
prison here. Last time i went there they
kept calling the cop's on me for when i
went to prison   plus i'am not ready to hurt
someone or get hurt   Such a predictment
Reason why i say wire the money to
western union now is the last few time's
i call you i could not get hold of you ok
But i will call you if i can get threw to you
on Monday the **16**th Aug   i **1/2** to catch
a bus out of here back to Anchorage n
report to a parole officer   so i don't kow
what time i will get back to Anchorage
they let me out at **9** in the mourning n
take me to the bus stop   I've been just
Drawing with Ink just practing. Today is
Sat **7** went outside this mourning   Finely
it sunny   Now it's count   **10:00**   sitting
here watching it get foggey again   look's
like rain again   Well i should get this
letter out   Call you when i get out   later
my frind   Take Care

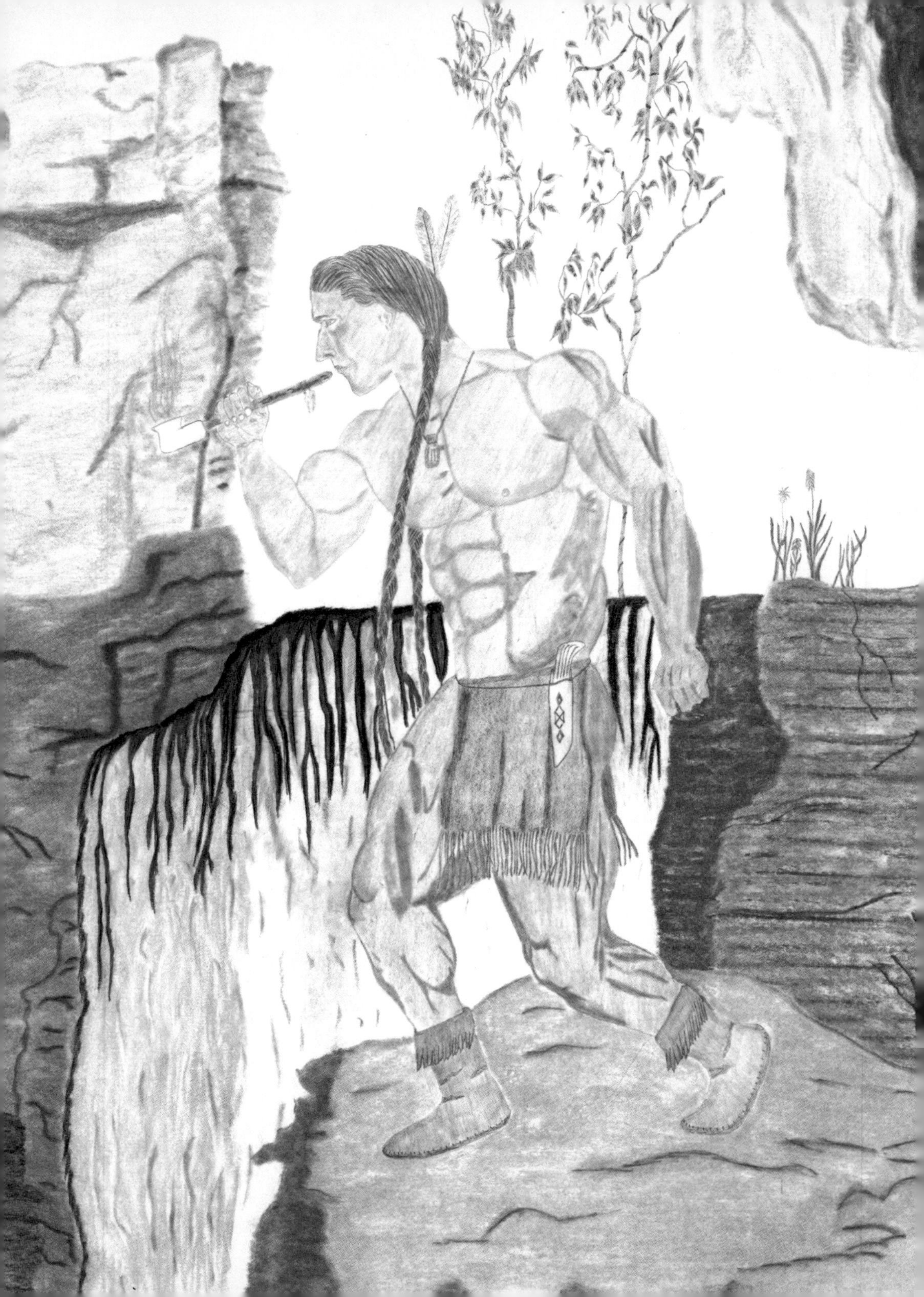

Martin had called me several time from the Alaskan Native Hospital. He had numerous health issues but now his congenital heart problems were starting to give him trouble. He took prescriptions for it but he would either forget to take it, lose it or somebody would steal it thinking it was some other drug. Each time he would be discharged he had no place to go. He'd worn out his welcome at Native friends' homes and even though he was promised a room in a shelter—something he despised more than the res— he could never quite get it; they had excuses at every turn. At least it was spring and he didn't have the Alaskan winter to deal with. He was broken and by all accounts it seemed he'd lost his will to live. No wonder. The last time I spoke to him he was back in the hospital:

March 25, 2016 (phone message)

Hey Gary, this is Martin...hey, where am I at?
[directed at nurse] What hospital? Which one?
"Alaskan Native"
What's my room number?
"221"
221...Do I have a phone number here?
"just call and ask for this room."
just call and ask for this room. Okay, Gary...I
got in here last night; I'd appreciate it, thank
you...bye, bye...take care brother [moaning]

(end of message)

June 6, 2016

I got a call from Anchorage informing me of Martin's death, asking me who I was and what I knew of him. They found him dead in the streets and the only thing he had was a piece of paper with my number. Regretfully, I said we were unrelated and suggested they contact the Yakama Nation. I always wanted to visit the Indian in Alaska. If only I had grasped the situation, I would've claimed the body of my "brother." How could they know? The story would be mine. After all, he had been adopted when he was a young boy. They just wanted to close the books on him anyway. I could have taken him to the woods and built a hanging cocoon for his sickly frame; beat the drum he gave me and chant 'til the sun went down. Lastly, I would put sage all around the improvised structure and cremate my friend; watch the smoke swirl towards the sky as if it were a singing spirit. As he had closed so many of his letters to me, "I'll let you go for now."

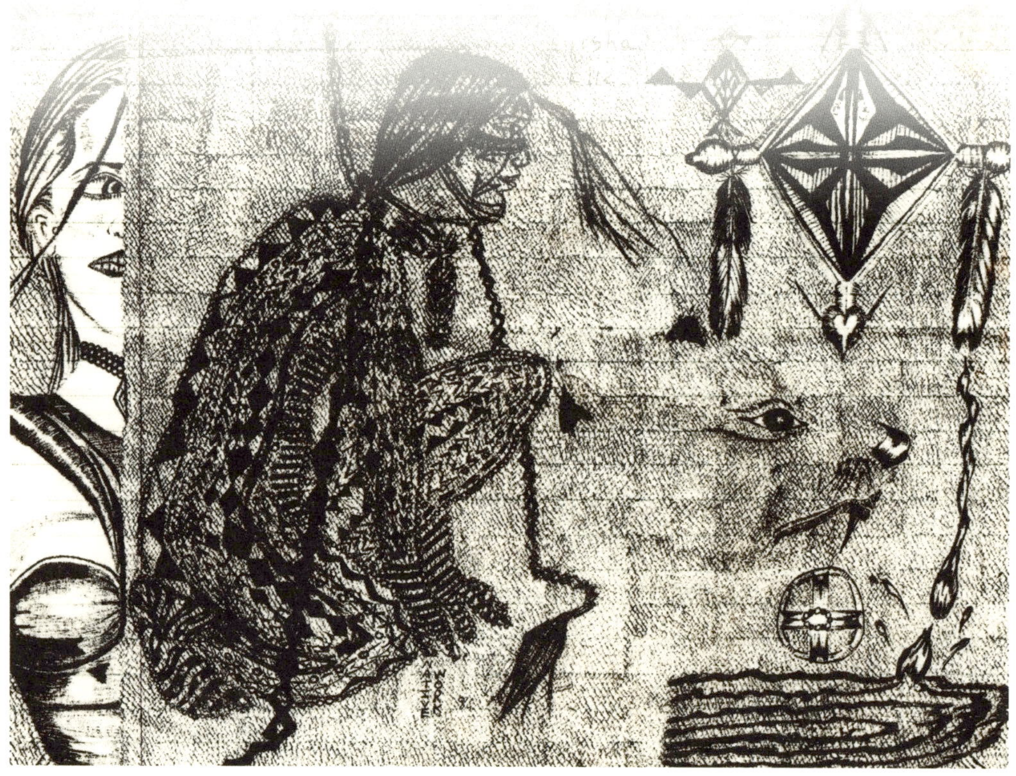

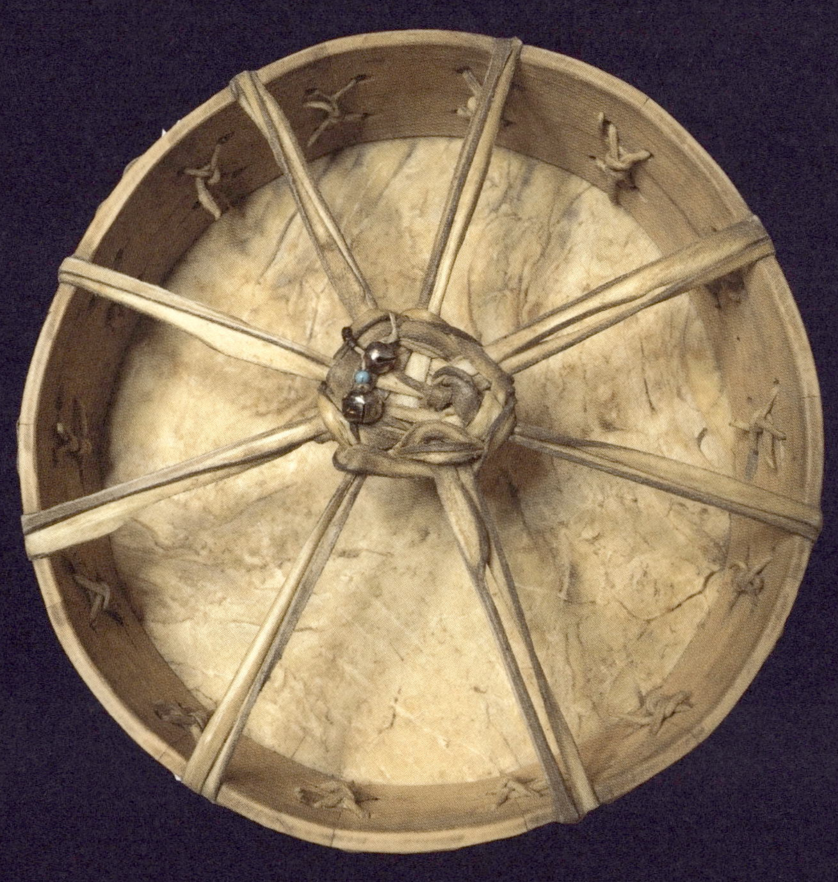

Artist unknown, Native American hand drum (back), circa 2000

GARY HILL
80 VINE ST. #101
SEATTLE, WA
9812
98121

FWD

MARTIN COTHREN
℅ BEAN'S CAFE
1101 E 3rd AVE.
ANCHORAGE, AK
99501

SEATTLE WA 980
04 JUN 2016 PM 7 L
USA FOREVER

Deceased
P.O Bx 265
Toppinish, WA
99501

NIXIE   992   SE 1   7206/   16
                                              FWD
RETURN TO SENDER
NOT DELIVERABLE AS ADDRESSED
UNABLE TO FORWARD
BC: 99503451301   *2326-01354-04-34

© DIS VOIR, 2021

www.disvoir.com

www.facebook/groups/disvoir

ISBN:978-2-914563-96-3

Printed by Petro Ofsetas, Lithuania, Europe